52 Mentor Musings

ALSO BY ROBIN COX

(more information available at www.yess.co.nz)

The Mentoring Spirit of the Teacher—Inspiration, support and guidance for aspiring and practicing teacher-mentors

Expanding the Spirit of Mentoring—Simple steps and fun activities for a flourishing peer mentor or peer support program

Nurturing the Spirit of Mentoring—50 fun activities for young people and for peer mentor training

Encouraging the Spirit of Mentoring—50 fun activities for the ongoing training of teacher-mentors, volunteer mentors, student leaders, peer mentors and youth workers

The Spirit of Mentoring—A manual for adult volunteers

Letter 2 a Teen—Becoming the Best I can Be

Making a Difference—The Teacher-Mentor, the Kids and the M.A.D Project

7 Key Qualities of Effective Teachers: Encouragement for Christian Educators

Mentoring Minutes: Weekly Messages to Encourage Anyone Working with Youth

The Barnabas Prayer: Becoming an Encourager in Your Community

CHOICES: Encouraging Youth to Achieve Greatness

MENTOR: Strategies to Inspire Young People

"If you're looking for an inspiring guide for anyone who 'moves alongside a young person as their non-judgmental cheerleader,' 52 *Mentor Musings* is it. Robin Cox distills decades of research and practice into relatable wisdom—sometimes packing it into a figurative paper bag. His 17-Point Personal Growth Kit transforms everyday objects into life lessons, like a rubber band (stay flexible) and an eraser (learn one lesson from every mistake). Practical and insightful—a valuable read!"

—**Magdalena Brzezinska**, Academic Instructor, WSB Merito University, Poznan, Poland

"Drawing on decades of mentoring experience, Robin brings together personal stories, practical strategies, and up-to-date research in 52 short, weekly messages. Whether you're a teacher, mentor, parent—or all three—this book is an invaluable companion you'll want within arm's reach. Easy to read and packed with wisdom, inspiration, and encouragement, it's a must-have for anyone walking alongside young people, helping them grow, set goals, and become the best version of themselves."

—**Trish Nees**, Teacher, New Zealand

"Through real-life stories—including surviving cancer and early personal tragedy—here is a powerful, authentic reflection on mentoring, resilience, and personal growth. The author offers practical, no-nonsense insights shaped by a lifetime of mentoring. Poignant yet grounded, each weekly chapter delivers accessible wisdom, making this a valuable read for anyone working with young people."

—**Chris Wright**, Board member, Presbyterian and Methodist Schools Association, Queensland, Australia

"These weekly lessons, stories, and case studies offer a wealth of information and inspiration for anyone who is mentoring a young person in their life. I found the advice offered here to be both deeply moving and energizing, reminding us that the act of mentoring can benefit us adults as much as the young people we care for."

—**Mike Garringer**, Senior Director of Research and Quality, Mentor USA

"In a society grappling with disconnection, Robin Cox's book is a much-needed resource for mentors, parents, educators, and others supporting young people in uncertain times. Each weekly reflection feels like a personal mentoring session—blending relatable stories, actionable insights, and genuine encouragement."

—**Jenny Horst**, CEO, Upside Youth Mentoring Aotearoa, New Zealand

"As our social media dependance increasingly draws us away from core values, core relationships, committed support systems, we need a warm book like this that offers wise counsel shaped by personal experiences in many different contexts, offering insight and proven approaches—and challenging questions! These nurture positive relations for which all people—young and old—are hankering."

—**Rudi Pakendorf**, Educator, Minnesota

"If the definition of 'teenager' is taken as meaning 'between ages'—i.e., the period between childhood and adulthood—then it would be true to say that Robin Cox's latest book, *52 Mentor Musings*, builds a bridge 'over the troubled water' of adolescence (thanks Simon and Garfunkel), and links the two ages of youth together. With the sincerity of his personal experiences, Robin continually emphasizes that the guide over this bridge needs to build up a wealth of compassion, trust, and understanding if a true connection is to be made. Building bridges for teenagers is a huge privilege rewarded when the mentor sees blossoming of confidence in the young person. These musings will breathe life into all who are privileged to work with young people."

—**Keith Richardson**, CEO, Principals Academy Trust, South Africa

"I highly recommend Robin Cox's latest book for those who seek to mentor, parent, and teach young men and women. He emphasizes that successful mentorship, like any other meaningful relationship, is built upon trust tested over time. He speaks with authority on the practical aspects of mentorship, and with humility on the gracious gifts and rewards of developing careful and caring relationships with young people.

—**Andrew Cook**, Retired Teacher, Cape Town, South Africa

"Wearing my senior's hat, I highly recommend 52 Mentor Musings as an insightful and inspiring resource—one to regularly 'dip into.' Packed with wisdom, it empowers young people to reach their potential and become compassionate contributors in an ever-changing world. A truly valuable read."

—**KAREN MACKAY**, Retired Teacher, New Zealand

"This timely offering by Robin Cox illuminates the power of human connection at the 'best' and the 'worst of times' for our youth. The vignette style of this book, interspersed with proven strategies, current research, true stories, and analogies kept me engaged. While I found it hard to put down, it is essentially, a 'read it when you need it,' must-have resource for all who journey with young people."

—**CARO EMSLIE**, Educator, Australia

"These musings are for everyone, mentors, teachers, employers included. Having two teenage children—and being a leader and mentor in a corporate workplace—I have found them invaluable."

—**EMMA HUGGETT**, South Africa

"Robin Cox's life's experiences, his strength in adversity from a life-threatening disease at an early age, and other cardinal factors in education, place him in a unique position to foster a greater knowledge for patience, perseverance, strength, and humility from educators. These and other topics—unlocking potential, celebrating strengths, providing practical strategies, engendering curiosity, and survival for challenging times—will surely equip all who journey alongside teenagers for their empowerment."

—**PAUL MURRAY**, Educator, South Africa

52 Mentor Musings

To Encourage Anyone *Motivating* Youth

ROBIN COX

RESOURCE *Publications* · Eugene, Oregon

52 MENTOR MUSINGS
To Encourage Anyone Motivating Youth

Copyright © 2025 Robin Cox. All rights reserved. Except for brief quotations in critical publications or reviews, no part of this book may be reproduced in any manner without prior written permission from the publisher. Write: Permissions, Wipf and Stock Publishers, 199 W. 8th Ave., Suite 3, Eugene, OR 97401.

Resource Publications
An Imprint of Wipf and Stock Publishers
199 W. 8th Ave., Suite 3
Eugene, OR 97401

www.wipfandstock.com

PAPERBACK ISBN: 979-8-3852-3672-5
HARDCOVER ISBN: 979-8-3852-3673-2
EBOOK ISBN: 979-8-3852-3674-9
VERSION NUMBER 04/23/25

Dedicated to the memory of my great friends
Hugh Huggett (1939–2024)
and
Peter Van Ryneveld (1956–2023)

> Friendship is the shadow of evening;
> it grows until the sun of life sets.
> —Jean de la Fonteine

Contents

Preface | xi
A Mentor's Dream | xiv

WEEK 1: I Nearly Gave Up on Emma and Am Glad that I Didn't | 1
WEEK 2: Life Lessons from Cancer: Finding Strength in Adversity | 7
WEEK 3: People Want to Connect with You. Do You Believe This? | 12
WEEK 4: Key Points for Successful Mentoring | 16
WEEK 5: High Anxiety: A Growing Concern | 19
WEEK 6: Developing More Resilient Teenagers in a Fast-Paced World | 22
WEEK 7: 'How Do I Know That You are Genuine? Can You Be Trusted?' | 27
WEEK 8: Life Skills—Be Coachable | 29
WEEK 9: 10 Life Lessons for a Purposeful Life | 32
WEEK 10: Five Proven Key Qualities of a Great Mentor | 37
WEEK 11: 'You Have the Seeds of Greatness Within You.' A Helpful Perspective | 40
WEEK 12: Boys Will be Boys! Embracing the Individuality of Young Minds | 43
WEEK 13: 'I am Tired of Living Like This. Please Help.' Mila's Story | 47
WEEK 14: Unlocking Potential: Supporting Teenagers to Set Personal Best Goals | 52
WEEK 15: How to Help Youth Achieve Personal Best Goals | 55
WEEK 16: The Importance of Patience and Perseverance in Reaching Your Goals | 58

CONTENTS

WEEK 17: 'Never Quit on Me!' Understand a Teenage Brain | 62

WEEK 18: Winning Ways to Achieve One's Potential | 66

WEEK 19: Practical Tips for Positive Parenting and Stress Management | 68

WEEK 20: 'She Helped Me Gain Self-Confidence...' Life-Changing Moments | 71

WEEK 21: 'No Words Can Express My Gratitude Towards You...' Reaching Out | 75

WEEK 22: One Day They Will Thank You | 78

WEEK 23: 'This Is Your Calling and Your Gift.' | 82

WEEK 24: 10 Proven Strategies to Become an Effective Mentor | 85

WEEK 25: The Power of Goal-Setting | 88

WEEK 26: The Transformative Power of Mentorship: Celebrating Influential Teachers | 91

WEEK 27: Controller, or a Positive Person of Influence? | 95

WEEK 28: How to Build a Resilient Youth | 99

WEEK 29: Build Meaningful Relationships | 104

WEEK 30: Life Lessons from Meeting a Nobel Peace Prize Winner | 107

WEEK 31: Mentoring Strategies Developed from My Life Journey | 111

WEEK 32: 'When It Comes Down to It, We All Just Want to Be Loved.' | 115

WEEK 33: Practical Strategies to Support Youth from High-Risk Environments | 120

WEEK 34: Two Key Words that Cost Us Nothing to Say, Yet Can Be Life-Changing | 124

WEEK 35: How to Encourage Others to Achieve Greatness | 128

WEEK 36: The Ultimate 17 Point Personal Growth Kit | 131

WEEK 37: Thoughts on Becoming a Positive Influencer | 134

WEEK 38: My Relationships Matter to Me | 137

WEEK 39: Proven Goal-Setting Tips: My Personal Experience | 141

WEEK 40: Exploring the Connection between Mentoring and Jigsaw Puzzles | 145

WEEK 41: Mentoring Lessons from the Olympic Games | 149

WEEK 42: Reflecting on Life's Meaning and Purpose | 154

WEEK 43: A Giant Leap of Faith, or a Moment of Madness? | 157
WEEK 44: Navigating Challenges in the Modern World | 161
WEEK 45: Invest Time in Life-Changing Decisions | 164
WEEK 46: Insights from a Helicopter Rescue: A
  Journey of Courage and Growth | 168
WEEK 47: 'If Only I Could Be a Better Parent . . . or
  Coach . . . or Friend . . .' | 171
WEEK 48: Secrets Shared for Living a Healthy
  and Balanced Lifestyle | 175
WEEK 49: To Love and Be Loved—Every Life Matters | 179
WEEK 50: Enjoying Positive, Life-Changing Relationships | 181
WEEK 51: With Thanks to an Olympian Who Changed My Life | 185
WEEK 52: Always Look for the Magical Moments | 189

Appendix 1: Mentoring Matters | 195
Acknowledgments | 197
Bibliography | 199

Preface

On 16 March 1999, at a Rotary function in Hamilton, New Zealand, I shared my education experiences, thoughts, and ideas about how to motivate young people to chase their dreams, and reach their potential.

After I had spoken, a 94-year-old retired teacher called me aside, and offered me this message of hope: "Some people have good ideas. Some have visions. Hold on to your vision. May God be with you."

I have done my best to heed his inspiring words.

These 52 weekly messages originated as a series of 150 blog posts, a collation of research linked to youth mentoring, and the education of adolescents and young adults.

The 2023 World Economic Forum's *The Future of Jobs Report* investigated how jobs and skills will evolve in the foreseeable future. The report highlighted some key skills, which are expected to increase in importance in the years ahead: cognitive skills—creative thinking and analytical thinking; self-efficacy—resilience; flexibility and agility; and technological literacy, which includes Artificial Intelligence (AI).[1]

Reports on the impact of the COVID-19 pandemic describe many of our young people as either feeling lost, or losing hope in the future. There has been an increase in anxiety levels, together with many expressions of pessimism about the future, a lack of motivation to participate in the activities they usually enjoy, and an increase in the number of young people reluctant to ask for help.

Clearly, there is a significant need for trusted adults to move alongside our young people—as their brains develop—to guide, motivate, and encourage them to move into the largely unknown and challenging future, with greater self-confidence, boldness, and courage.

1. World Economic Forum, *The Future of Jobs Report*.

When youth are focused and in a positive or controlled emotional state, their executive functions in the prefrontal cortex organize newly coded memories into long-term knowledge more successfully.[2]

Parents, educators, and volunteer mentors are busy people. These *weekly* messages are designed to be an encouragement and support to all who journey alongside our young people during their confusing adolescent years, a user-friendly reminder of the important mentoring, parenting, and teaching skills, and strategies that can transform lives.

Researchers Karen Reivich and Andrew Shatte highlight an important point anyone guiding youth can remember, and which is touched on in many of these musings: "Behavioral criticism points to problem solving; character criticism stymies it."[3]

These messages include true stories to give credibility to the research—names of students have been changed to protect their privacy—and to show that there are a variety of mentoring approaches, dependent on the environment in which mentees are living.

The *weekly* messages will equip mentors with knowledge, skills, and strategies for the mentoring journey. The messages are arranged within a holistic framework—the development of the *whole* person.

A variety of topics are explored, which are linked to the promotion of the key skills required for the future, as mentioned in the World Economic Forum report. These include self-image; the impact of technology on young people; resiliency; goal-setting; effective communication; values; how to resolve conflicts using a positive mindset, and the role of family and other networks in the lives of young people.

I have included a number of my personal experiences to facilitate the reader's understanding both of the value of sharing life lessons with mentees, and also as examples of true stories which young people value.

This book has *not* been written as a book to read from cover to cover in one sitting. Readers who want more detailed and daily information about young people, could refer to my recent book, *Mentoring Minutes: Weekly Messages to Encourage Anyone Guiding Youth*, which could serve as a companion to this book.

The messages in this book are arranged to cover topics like those mentioned above, and as they are *weekly* messages, repetition is deliberate.

2. Cox, *CHOICES*, 80.
3. Reivich and Shatte, *The Resilience Factor*, 273.

Ancient Greek philosopher Aristotle stated: "We are what we repeatedly do. Excellence then, is not an act but a habit."

The messages vary in length. I would encourage readers to keep the book in an easily accessible place—on an office or work desk, or by their bed—so they can set a short time aside each week to refresh their thinking, and deepen their understanding of the spirit of mentoring.

Early in my teaching career, I came across these inspiring words written by American author and educator John Holt, to encourage anyone guiding young people:

> We can think of ourselves not as teachers, but as gardeners. A gardener does not grow flowers; he tries to give them what he thinks will help them grow by themselves. A child's mind, like a flower, is a living thing. We can't make it grow by sticking things onto it any more than we can make a flower grow by gluing on leaves and petals. All we can do is surround the growing mind with what it needs for growing and have faith that it will take what it needs and grow.

Thank you for reading this book. My hope is that it will motivate, inspire, encourage, and equip more people as they develop positive, and meaningful relationships with young people in the knowledge that *every life matters*.

Robin Cox
New Zealand

A Mentor's Dream

My dream for you [my mentee] is that you wake up each morning, look at yourself in the mirror, love from the heart the person you see, always strive to be your unique self, and take a positive attitude into every day.

My dream for you is that you build your life on strong foundations, so that you can withstand the inevitable storms of life, and remain a positive person.

My dream for you is that you dare to dream big dreams, set realistic, achievable, and measurable goals, fail sometimes, but remain determined to conquer adversity, and to discover, develop, and use your special gifts and talents to bring about a better community, a more caring society, a more compassionate world.

My dream for you is that you often take time out to reflect on your progress, to visualize yourself ten years from now as a happy, proud, yet humble person, content with life, continually placing the interests of others before your own.

My dream for you is that you discover the meaning of true love; that you sensibly risk entering into positive and meaningful relationships with others, and that your life is wonderfully enriched as a consequence.

My dream for you is that you remember that you are a beautiful person both on the inside and the outside; that you have potential greatness within you, and that, as you leave your footprints on the sands of life's journey, many will walk positively after you, and strive to emulate all that you achieve as a positive person of influence.

My dream for you is that you always remember that you are a special person in God's eyes, and that you discover, during your life's journey, His unique purpose for placing you on this planet.

My dream for you is everything that you positively wish for yourself![1]

1. Cox, *MENTOR*, xviii.

WEEK 1

I Nearly Gave Up on Emma and Am Glad that I Didn't

Realize that your ability to care for someone is one of your greatest assets.

Patience and perseverance can change someone's life.

Have you ever felt like quitting on a person of any age you care about? Maybe, at times, even your own rebellious child? Do you ever feel like you are hitting your head against a brick wall?

I certainly have had these thoughts, though my passion to encourage teenagers to reach their potential has led me to try *anything* to encourage them to make some positive choices.

Emma's true story—parts of which I have shared in my other mentoring books—can encourage mentors during the mentoring journey.

Seventeen-year-old Emma was a young girl I mentored a few years ago. She had a volatile temper, which her peers knew. There were many times her peers pushed that anger button to get a reaction. And, when she reacted, the language was vile, a fairly sure sign of a young girl who lacked self-confidence.

Underneath this angry and tough exterior though, I was quick to discover, was a wonderfully caring individual who would make sacrifices for others, and expect nothing in return. An example of this was the way she purchased a snack for a peer she did not know well who had left their money at home, and was attending an event at the place where Emma did casual work.

Emma refused to see a counselor, was shocking at her management of time, a great procrastinator, and did not believe in setting goals because she had convinced herself she would never achieve any of them.

I was asked by a colleague to have a chat with her, as the situation was becoming serious. Emma's antisocial behavior had become disruptive, and some colleagues believed she would be better off completing her schooling elsewhere.

Emma was happy to chat to me, and I was comfortable for her to control the content and direction of the chat.

I asked her permission to make some notes while we introduced ourselves. She was happy with that. I also told her that our conversations would remain confidential—within school policies and procedures. We began a journey, best described as a fascinating and unpredictable emotional roller-coaster.

The focus was simple. Emma would set some realistic, achievable performance goals for her academic subjects. I would monitor her progress, and take on the role of a non-judgmental cheerleader.

The key to this process, as I kept explaining to her, was that *she* set the goals, and she made the choices. We had to ensure the personal best goals were realistic, and Emma had to learn the meaning of being accountable for her choices.

I continually reminded Emma, when she slipped up, that Rome was not built in a day, and to persevere, so she heard a consistent and positive message from me.

At one of our meetings early on our journey, I shared a wonderful description someone had written of a young person that spoke to their inner and outer beauty. I personalized it for Emma, and told her that *that* was the person with whom I was communicating.

I gave her a copy for her own reference. She didn't say much that day, though I know she was appreciative, and smiled her thanks. A small, yet significant step in making a connection with Emma in a non-threatening, and caring way.

As the months rolled on and Emma stumbled and fell, stood up again, failed to meet a deadline, was in more trouble—yes, there was a fairly consistent pattern of behavior—another relationship developed, this time between Emma and my personal assistant, Ruth, who was also the mum of teenage children.

Emma would often pop in just to say "hello" to Ruth. Emma clearly felt safe and secure in this particular school environment.

Ruth and I sat down one day and worked out some strategies in our work with Emma. We made sure that Emma could not play one of us off against the other, which she was smart enough to do.

There were days, for example, when Emma might try and avoid a lesson and pop up to our work area to have a chat to Ruth. Ruth would chat to Emma for five minutes and then remind her that she needed to head to class. Emma mumbled and Ruth, always with a smile, told Emma that she would tell me that Emma had missed a lesson. That was not the message Emma wanted to hear, so she would quickly head off to class.

One day Emma left a class feeling angry that the teacher was picking on her, had her favorites, and Emma was being blamed for something she hadn't done, while others were not being pulled up for their behavior.

Emma rushed up to our work area, and was ranting and raving to Ruth.

I called Emma into my office, closed the glass door (important for safety and security reasons that people could see into my office) and told her that, rather than rant and rave in a public area, it would be better for her if she walked into my office, got everything off her chest, and didn't hurt anyone else by saying something she might later regret.

I pulled out a picture of the brain and asked her permission to share something about how her brain operated when she was that emotional. She was genuinely interested in this.

My aim was to develop strategies to avoid these outbursts, such as, take a deep breath and count *slowly* to twenty. I encouraged her to appreciate that she was making choices and every choice had a consequence.

Later I spoke with her about her swearing. I told her that I did not really appreciate swearing at any time though, if that was how she had to express herself at that time, it was okay.

She would walk into my office, rant and rave, and I would just sit listening, using eye contact and positive body language.

One day she challenged me and asked why I wasn't saying anything? I simply smiled and said, "I am listening to you and trying to understand how you are feeling."

Then she moved to a point where, after a silence, she would calm down and say, "Sorry, sir."

That was her apology for swearing, or for making unnecessary and damning comments about a teacher or a peer which I was encouraging her to stop doing.

Emma would smile and visibly relax, and we would continue to work on strategies to improve her anger management.

On a few occasions, after our discussion, she would head off to find her teacher and apologize for her behavior. Emma was developing her self-confidence, and becoming a more positive and resilient person. The lion heart within was being tamed.

Emma possessed some sporting—and musical—talent. I would make a point of watching some of her matches on a Saturday morning whenever I could. I had coached the sport she was playing, so was able to offer some technical coaching tips, and congratulate her efforts when she had performed admirably during a match.

It was a point of common ground and often a useful conversation starter, especially when our paths crossed in the school grounds.

Emma had a wicked sense of humor. Ruth, Emma and I had plenty of laughs, especially when Emma was all wound up, had relaxed, chilled for a little, and had gathered herself into a calmer place.

There were days when it was easy to give up with Emma. Assessments not completed, silly behavior getting her into trouble, and a whole lot more. Emma knew that, without consistent work, she was unlikely to pursue her career interests which involved helping others.

I did some work on sourcing the requirements for the career she was interested in, and sat with her one day going through the qualifications needed on the university website (she had also done this prior to talking to me, an encouraging sign).

Emma didn't believe she was going to obtain the results she needed. I reassured her that, if she was prepared to work consistently, I genuinely believed she could achieve the desired results. Emma was also aware that I had contacted her teachers, and asked them to keep me informed if she was falling behind, or did not meet deadlines.

We continued to refer back to her goals, and adjust them up or down as she developed a more consistent approach to her academic studies, so they remained achievable and realistic.

I NEARLY GAVE UP ON EMMA AND AM GLAD THAT I DIDN'T

Occasionally I would send Emma an email of encouragement, reminding her to meet the deadlines, and why she needed to do this. When she performed superbly in a test on one occasion, a special moment occurred, as my email reminded her that she could achieve her dreams with consistent effort.

I wanted to put that in writing as well as verbalize it. I was speaking to the potential she was not always able to see. Sometimes she acknowledged the email, often not, though she always told me she had read it, which was all that mattered to me.

I was drip-feeding a message that was basically saying, "I believe in you!" I hoped these positive messages would impact her developing brain and growth mindset in encouraging ways.

Emma made it through to the end of her final year at school which surprised many who thought the school might be forced to ask her to leave. She had supportive parents, although I wasn't always comfortable that they knew how best to encourage her to reach her potential.

On her last day at school Emma popped in to see me to thank me for all my support, and for putting up with her outbursts and inconsistent behavior. She gave me a lovely engraved Parker pen, an expensive bottle of wine, and a card.

On one side of the pen was my name and on the other a heart-shaped symbol and her name "Emma." She gave Ruth an identical gift. The pen remains one of my treasured possessions, a reminder that every young person is unique, has gifts and talents to be nurtured, and I must *never* quit on them.

However, it was the content of the card that was touching.

> Thank you for helping me get through school. I guess school just wasn't really my thing. I really appreciate all the time that you gave up to ensure I attended classes, got my work done, that I was on the right track with my life and so much more! Thank you for inspiring me to be a better person. You give me hope that I will still have a chance in life when I graduate with a result that reflects not even half of my potential. I don't think I can express enough how grateful I am for everything you do for me, even if I don't always show it. But, most of all, thank you so much for never ever giving up on me and always pushing me to achieve my best. You have made me a better person.

A few years after Emma had left school, she connected with me on a social media platform. It had been some years since she and I had last chatted. She had obtained a university degree, and was loving the work she was doing. She concluded her message to me:

> I think often about what you and other caring teachers did for me at the [school], which has shaped the person I have become today. My mum is always on my case telling me to write a letter to update you all. If you weren't so patient with me, I would never have been able to pursue my dream career. Thank you for everything you did!

There are many times when we are like the parachutist or sky diver taking a novice for a ride. We have to control the parachute, and do our best to ensure that we land safely at our destination, no matter how choppy or gusty the wind, or how risky the ride might be. We have to display calmness, perseverance, tolerance, unconditional love and grace, and speak into the future our novice cannot yet see. That is the spirit of mentoring.

WEEK 2

Life Lessons from Cancer: Finding Strength in Adversity

Believe in miracles. They happen every day.

"*Robin is dangerously ill,*" my father wrote in his journal.

At the age of nine, I was diagnosed with cancer of the jaw, and given months to live. I wasn't told at the time that I had cancer, nor was I told that I only had a five percent chance of survival.

My parents initially thought I had mumps. When the swelling did not go down, I was sent to a specialist, and then underwent a biopsy. My parents were informed that I had bone cancer and would need radiation therapy. The worst-case scenario was that, without the radiation therapy, I probably only had a few months to live.

I missed more than a term of school while I had the radiation therapy followed by my first major operation. My mother took me to the hospital every day for two months. Many years later I discovered that I was receiving more than 2.5 times the normal dose of radiation therapy given to an adult, as the doctors were concerned about the possibility of the cancer spreading through my body.

I remember attending Groote Schuur Hospital in Cape Town, famous as the venue for the first heart transplant, and having this special mask molded to cover my face, being wheeled into the tunnel of a large machine, and having to lie still for however long. I don't remember all the details, although I was afraid, and dreaded hospital visits. Radiation therapy made me tired, and I had to take things carefully.

After the radiation therapy was completed, the swelling had reduced, and the doctors decided to operate and remove what was left of the cancerous tumor. During the next couple of years, I underwent two major operations, the first to remove the cancerous jawbone and some lymph nodes, the second to graft a rib which would grow as my new jawbone.

The hope was that, once I had stopped growing and my face had adapted to this new jawbone, I would be as near normal in looks as was possible, and the final plastic surgery would cover the hollow in my cheek as a result of the operation.

During the next few years, through to the end of my senior school years, I made regular trips to the outpatient clinic at the hospital, my significant memory being the healing hands of the amazing specialists who treated me.

I recall the day I returned to junior school after my first major operation, and had to sit in the car until after assembly. The headmaster told the school that I was returning, was disfigured, yet needed to be treated normally. Many of my teachers reached out to me, encouraged and moved alongside me in different ways, and at different times.

Their acts of kindness impacted my life in a significant way, so much so that I decided, at the age of about eleven, that I wanted to be a teacher.

One occasion during my junior school years, which I remember as though it was only yesterday, was being called out of my class by the headmaster before lunch, and told that my father was coming to fetch my brother and me.

My mother had undergone an operation and was in hospital. My father had been called to the hospital early that morning. As we clambered into the car, we heard that my mother had died from a pulmonary embolism.

My father took us to the beach that afternoon, but there was a silence, a sadness—possibly we all just felt numb. I didn't feel like swimming, nor exploring the rock ponds which I loved doing at that age. The family had to adapt to my mother's sudden and untimely death.

After many tantrums and tears, I was allowed to play sports again. I developed a way to cope with my disfigurement through my involvement in sports, and my discovery that I had some talent.

About eighteen months after my mother died, my father married a close family friend of my godparents, a divorcee, who had suffered the tragedy of losing her son who was my age (and blind in one eye), when he was hit by a car as he ran across a busy road to watch a helicopter land on a large common close to a children's hospital. My step-sister was a little younger than me.

This marriage changed the dynamics within our family. My older teenage brother and sister battled to accept two new people into the family. No matter how hard she tried, my step-mother could never replace my mother. It took her a long time to understand this.

Meanwhile, I journeyed through the confusing adolescent years, lacking in self-confidence, having to put up with the never-ending stares of young and old to remind me of my disfigurement, and the occasional hurtful comments from my peers.

I was shy and an introvert within a family experiencing what can only be described as "interesting dynamics."

During the dark times I would ask, "Why me?" and feel filled with self-pity, though I had a way out of these feelings because I learnt how to change my inner narrative and make new choices.

My passion to play sports kept me going. I also joined a youth group for a while, following my brother there, but all the other members of the group were at other schools and knew each other. Cliques were formed, and I was unable to break into any of these (not that I tried that hard), so I felt awkward, isolated, and eventually stopped attending.

When I was about fifteen, I withdrew into myself, and became a loner for about eighteen months. I shared little about how I was feeling with my family, kept to myself, and stayed at school as late as I possibly could playing sports.

During this time, I built a wall around myself, not letting anyone into my most private thoughts, though I don't actually recall more than a couple of people (both girls of my age) trying to get in.

I concluded that, because I was different from everyone else, I would need to prove myself. I set some personal sport goals, made many sacrifices, and trained hard. I was appointed to leadership positions at school, and captained teams; gained state colors in cricket, field hockey, and cross-country, and also represented my school in squash racquets, and badminton.

And that was how I gained the respect of both peers and teachers, which had been one of my goals. I didn't want people to feel sorry for me because of my physical disability, and I don't think they did.

Some of my sport coaches became my mentors, one of these being my headmaster, himself a former international cricketer. I was like a sponge with these people, forever asking questions, and wanting to learn more. I didn't realize at the time that they were shaping my character, and helping me create a value base on which I would build the rest of my life.

As school captain in my final year, my headmaster taught me much about leadership, the importance of standing up and being counted, leading by example, and how to persist through tough times.

I returned from a successful under nineteen interstate cricket festival, and had my final plastic surgery operation to complete the rebuilding of my face. However, later that year I made the tough decision to stop playing competitive sport as there were too many risks involved.

I felt shattered for a while, and then chose, once again, to change my inner narrative and turn all my sporting goals into coaching goals, all of which I achieved in the years that followed. I graduated from university and taught for over forty years, during which time I married and we had two children, but that is a story for another day.

It took me a long time to share my story. Who would ever believe that a nine-year-old boy facing death from cancer, would one day be offered six publishing contracts within five years to write six books promoting the spirit of mentoring, and encouraging others to become positive people of influence in their community?

Each of us has a story to share with young people we guide, an opportunity to share life lessons as a way of encouraging them to find meaning and purpose to their lives.

10 LIFE LESSONS FROM MY CANCER JOURNEY

There are a multitude of lessons I learned from my adolescent experiences which I have shared with many students, teachers, and parents over the years to encourage them when they were facing tough challenges.

About fourteen years ago I had my thyroid removed—as a result of the radiation all those years ago—and more traces of cancer were found and removed. Will it return? No matter, I will change the inner narrative accordingly, and remember the following lessons I have learnt from my life experiences.

1. The choices I make, particularly about my attitude to life, define who I am. My life mantra: There *is* a solution to every problem.
2. I wake up each day thankful for the opportunities to spread a message of *hope*.
3. Find people who believe in me, and see the potential which I often can't see, to be my cheerleaders.
4. Set and chase my personal best goals; enjoy the triumph of hard achievement, and turn obstacles into opportunities.
5. Continue to develop a lifelong habit of supporting the underdog, the hurting, and the broken, because I have been there, and can empathize with their pain.
6. Ask for help—it took me quite some time to do this—and remember that to be vulnerable is a strength, and not a weakness.
7. Develop ways to use my God-given gift of encouragement to make a small difference in the world, especially in my interactions with teenagers, teachers, and volunteer adult mentors.
8. Never fear failure—it took me time to learn this—and to have the courage to stay true to my values no matter the cost;
9. My coaches and encouragers modeled the importance of believing in oneself, backing oneself, and striving to fulfil one's potential with humility.
10. Always retain a healthy sense of humor—which includes being able to laugh at myself, and not taking life too seriously—and live a healthy and balanced lifestyle.

I live with a sense of gratitude to my family, doctors, teachers, mentors, and close friends who encouraged me to fulfil my potential which often I could not see.

The spirit of mentoring encourages others to be grateful for the many blessings they experience even when dealing with tough challenges.

Maybe you have a story of overcoming adversity to encourage those you mentor?

WEEK 3

People Want to Connect with You. Do You Believe This?

See every moment as a precious gift.

Who are the people who have made a positive influence in your life? I recall some teachers and coaches, especially those who moved alongside me during my cancer journey as a young boy—amazing people.

Do you ever think about the people who have mentored you at some point in your life, especially during your young and formative years? How old were you at the time?

There is a significant demand for mentors for our young people in the global community.

Young people have much power, though are journeying through one of the most confusing times in their lives. With the support of a trusted adult, they can be effectively empowered to make a positive difference in their communities as they strive to reach their potential.

A few months ago, as I was thinking more about the key qualities of a mentor as a friend, my wife and I flew to Cape Town to participate in a memorial gathering for my closest friend Pete, to whom I have dedicated this book.

Pete was a successful businessman, visionary, philanthropist, conservationist, mentor, and idealistic dreamer (like me) with whom I had communicated for fifty-one years. As teenagers we set out to change the world. Pete had achieved so much before his untimely death. Our friendship was unique, and his death has left a significant void in my life.

Pete had been diagnosed with a brain tumor about eight weeks earlier. He entered a local hospital for a biopsy, and never recovered consciousness. Doctors discovered stage four cancer spreading like a wild fire.

Pete had been a friend and mentor to many people, especially those living in disadvantaged areas in southern Africa.

He generously shared his expertise, gave many a hand up, and spent hours listening, sharing life experiences, and encouraging a variety of people from different cultures and ethnicities to reach their potential.

Pete was an enthusiastic supporter of my writing, especially as I had many doubts about my writing ability, and he generously praised the news of an impending new book—which was published in 2024—shortly before his death. I am grateful that Pete and I had an opportunity to share thoughts about this book, though I am sad that he was unable to read one of the drafts and offer his feedback.

What follows is an extract from the book *MENTOR, Strategies to Inspire Young People*[1] to encourage mentors to appreciate the power of a positive connection with those they mentor.

MENTORS ARE FRIENDS

Friendship is at the core of your relationship with your mentee, though this depends on the type of relationship you enjoy with your mentee.

There is a difference, for example, between the volunteer adult mentor who is part of a youth mentoring program, and the more professional relationship between a teacher and a student. The teacher would adapt some of these qualities in line with their profession.

> *Fun-loving*—Have lots of fun together, as young people tend to have a wonderful sense of humor. Model what it means to laugh at yourself. Coach your mentee not to take themselves or life too seriously. Michael Karcher moves this thinking to a deeper, more holistic level:
>
>> Play is the best way to enter the world of a young person—no matter what age—because doing that extends a sign of respect

---

1. Cox, *MENTOR*, 18–21.

to youth. Mentors empower people, embolden them, encourage them, and respect them by being playful, because youth know that's their zone.... What is universal, very healthy, and good to encourage across both genders is the desire to create. Creation in many forms is equivalent to playing in the traditional sense.[2]

Respectful*—Respect both your mentees and yourself as unique beings of great self-worth with a positive self-image. Acknowledge the right of your mentees to make choices, and show them that their opinions and ideas are valued and matter.

Integrity—Be authentic and honest at all times. Be consistent and show up on time; be upright, reliable, and committed to the relationship, someone your mentees can depend on.

Empathetic*—Place yourself in the shoes of your mentees in order to understand them better. Try to understand *how* your mentee is feeling. Model empathy, and coach your mentee *how* to express empathy in their relationships with family, friends, and other members of the community. Your understanding helps you inspire them to greatness, or to reach their full potential. Educator Paul Browning explains: "listening at its best is a selfless act. It is about the other person and not you. It is about entering their world and seeing it from their viewpoint."[3]

Nurturing—Create a supportive relationship in which your mentees feel cared for, affirmed, and encouraged. Key features in establishing this relationship include being an *effective listener* with a non-judgmental attitude; commit to your mentees; believe in them; be accessible to them, and give of yourself unconditionally.

Developmental—Encourage your mentees to become the people *they* wish to be, a process that takes time, and requires patience, perseverance, and the understanding that developing a friendship also takes time. No "saviors" or "quick fixes" are needed.

Sincere*—Be yourself at all times; be genuine. That is, be aware of your innermost thoughts and feelings, accept them and, when appropriate, share them responsibly (self-expression); know yourself (self-awareness); and accept yourself (self-acceptance). Model a spirit of

2. Karcher, *Becoming a Better Mentor.*
3. Browning, *Principled,* 38.

selfless service—serving others, and expecting nothing in return, and as Albert Einstein shares: "Strive not to be a success, but rather to be of value."

* These are the key qualities, or the foundation stones of *any* meaningful relationship.

Pete was a wonderful and empathetic role model who displayed these qualities as he reached out to others. He was compassionate and caring, which is why so many people responded to his genuine interest in their life stories. He was an excellent listener, with a great sense of humor. He volunteered his time, and always seemed available to reach out to someone in need either when asked to share his expertise, or if he saw a particular need to which he felt competent to respond.

Have you any experiences as a mentor to share?

WEEK 4

Key Points for Successful Mentoring

See age as not a number, but how you feel inside.

Some time ago, I heard that a young man I mentored in the late 1980s had passed away from an incurable illness in 2017. I don't know any details, and I am still saddened that Nick is no longer with us.

Nick was a young man of courage and immense talent who came from a disadvantaged background, yet developed strengths that allowed him to fearlessly stand out from the crowd in an apartheid South Africa.

Nick helped me plan and organize non-racial symposia. He had an amazing sense of humor, developed superb leadership skills, and taught me so much about what a non-racial South Africa might look like.

News of his death brought many memories flooding back, and I shared his story in my book, *MENTOR, Strategies to Inspire Young People*.

This led me to reflect more on the power of mentoring, though mostly in relation to other students who crossed my path over the years. I wondered what they are doing with their lives today, and what might have been had they had the opportunity to be mentored when they were fifteen or sixteen years of age—unique gifts and talents to be nurtured and encouraged by a non-judgmental cheerleader.

So, it's probably a good time to share some of the key points I stress during the training of volunteer mentors:

KEY POINTS FOR SUCCESSFUL MENTORING

- The role of a mentor is *not* to fix students or families.
- Avoid the trap of getting too emotionally involved—it's not good for either party.
- Mentors are friends, not saviors, or rescuers.
- Don't fall into the trap of wanting to keep coming up with solutions, offering advice, or solving your mentees' problems for them. The most effective mentoring is guiding them to solve their own problems after brainstorming with you. This might take time, and does not have to happen immediately. For example, when talking about an issue, suggest: "Let's explore your options. What are they?" "Hey, maybe we can chat more about this, and then work out some plans for next year . . ." "Why don't you see what you can find out, and then we can chat again next week?"
- Consider using a journal to record your key conversation points if you are not already doing so.
- Keep exploring ways of encouraging your mentee to connect with the school—activities they can get involved in, what needs to be done, or what their priorities could be. You might even want to browse the school website yourself to see what's on offer.
- Keep sowing the seeds of positive peer pressure as you encourage your mentee to chase their dreams, and reach their potential.
- What's going on in their lives at this age? Remember how you felt as you were going through those confusing teenage years—most mentees are battling with self-image, or self-concept issues, despite a possible outward show of bravado, and an "I'm ok," attitude. At the same time don't look for, or create problems if they are not there.
- Find out in your discussions who the positive people are in their lives. For example, ask them: "If you were desperate for accommodation, or needed $100, who would you approach?" "Your parents—great! And who else?" This encourages talk about building that web of support around themselves for the future, communicating with people who believe in them, role models, and other potential wise guides.
- Work out an effective strategy regarding the use of email, or sending text messages to remain in touch, though have clear boundaries in place. Sometimes just a quick word of encouragement is all that's

needed. Or, if your mentee is feeling low, arrange for them to contact you in a day or two just to check on how things are going—short and sweet, always effective.

- Vary how you spend your time with your mentee. For example, you might go for a walk and talk, then spend fifteen minutes googling something on the computer and chatting. Boys prefer *doing* rather than sitting and just chatting—all will appreciate variety.
- Never hesitate to get in touch with program staff—where relevant—if there is something you need to discuss, no matter how trivial you think it might be.

The importance of the development of meaningful relationships in the lives of our young people is even more important in the digital age in which we are living, when face-to-face relationships might be lacking the depth to make them more meaningful.

Young people need guidance with regard to understanding body language, and how to verbalize their hopes and fears.

Where there are absent parents or the family isn't functioning too well, it is easier to understand why mentoring research continually points to the importance of a young person having at least three significant adults in their adolescent lives. Someone needs to be there for them during these formative years of their education.

Remember to speak to the potential you can see in any young person with whom you are communicating. You might just light a spark of hope that ignites slumbering dreams.

I recall asking Nick to share his story with students at the school where I was a school principal. You could have heard a pin drop as Nick, who by this stage had completed his university degree and had entered the workforce, inspired students to grasp every moment of their education, and never to accept a second-rate effort. A great man sadly missed, and I cherish the memories of our time together.

How are you creating cherished memories with the young people with whom you interact?

WEEK 5

High Anxiety: A Growing Concern

Be committed, determined, and disciplined—actions critical to success.

While I was walking along the beach one morning, I was mindful of the different shapes and sizes of footprints of others who had gone ahead of me. I reflected on the fact that the choices we make heavily impact our footprints on the sands of time.

I recalled walking around the school I taught at one day, and stumbling into a conversation between two final year students.

"I only had four hours sleep," said an animated Jess, "and this is my fourth cup of coffee!"

"Make sure you have nine hours sleep a night throughout the next week," I interjected. "Your brain needs time to consolidate your learning, and to discard what you don't need to remember."

"You won't be able to remember anything if you don't get your sleep," level-headed Rory added.

"I have so much to learn!" Jess was startled at my suggestion.

"How have you done through the semester?" I asked. "Have you been working consistently?"

Jess nodded.

"Then you will be fine," I reassured her, "but you need your sleep."

Jess was clearly on a caffeine high at the time, a bubbly personality, yet unable to hide the anxiety. I wondered if she was being placed under pressure to perform by her parents, or by her peers.

"At least you have a good sense of humor," I smiled.

"Sense of humor?" Jess looked puzzled. "That is not going to help me pass my exam."

As I listened to comments like those, I appreciated more and more how important it is for parents, students, and teachers to work together to ensure situations like this do not occur.

How many times do you stop each week and wonder where time has gone? Or mope about saying, "I don't have enough time," or "I am too busy!" or words to that effect?

What is causing the increased anxiety we see amongst our young people? How well had Jess planned and organized her time? Was she having nine hours sleep a night to allow her brain to process what was, and what was not worth storing?

Sixteen-year-old Jason once told me that one of his problems was that he did not finish his assessments on time. This was partly because he worked better in the subjects which he enjoyed, rather than those he either found irrelevant or boring, and partly because he clearly needed guidance with regard to organizing his schedule, and managing his time more effectively.

Our conversation ended up exploring hours of sleep, his personal best goals, and a breakdown of how he travelled through each day of the week.

Jason required a healthy and balanced lifestyle to reach his potential.

I stressed to him, by way of encouragement, that he needed a schedule that allowed him social time to be with his peers, or time simply to relax—important in the life of a teenager.

> It has scientifically been shown that if we continually ask our brains to switch back and forth between tasks, we waste time, make more mistakes, and remember less of what we've done.
> —Hector Garcia and Francesc Miralles[1]

Promoting the spirit of mentoring involves guiding young people on how to plan their days and weeks, encouraging them to identify different *qualities* of time, and adapting their behavior to suit each one.

Jason and I looked at the following three qualities of time:

---

1. Garcia and Miralles, *Ikigai*.

1. During *peak performance* hours the brain is functioning at maximum level. Teenagers can focus on the academic areas that require a high level of concentration. For example, they might revise for a test or exam, or work through a tough problem-solving task.
2. Certain times are *creative*. At such times, teenagers can allow their ideas to flow freely, as they are thinking clearly. They can write or design something, pursue a hobby, or read. The key is to stay motivated to study, or pursue the development of a life skill.
3. *Off-peak hours* bring fatigue. These times can be more constructive than many teenagers appreciate. For example, they can use such times to file or write notes, carry out chores or duties at home, or do whatever administrative work they need to do.

We explored different options and, during the next couple of weeks, Jason experimented with his schedule until he found what worked best for him.

Not only did his schedule become a game-changer for him, but he also removed some stress from his life, learnt to cope and deal with other challenges, and eventually graduated successfully from school, and moved on to study his career choice at university.

I ticked off some checkpoints to look out for in a young person being nurtured and mentored, as I observed Jason's progress:

- a greater sense of belonging;
- a better perspective of himself;
- a sense of hope for the future;
- a stronger sense of self-worth;
- a feeling of significance.

While one can take online courses to learn what one needs to do to improve in some areas, students value the face-to-face relationships with a wise guide on the side—a mentor, a parent, a teacher, a coach—someone they trust to help them develop strategies that will work for them; to talk through frustrations, challenges, and other teenage issues.

May *all* students find someone to take on that supportive role so they can create some wonderful footprints with the gifts and talents they have to offer.

WEEK 6

Developing More Resilient Teenagers in a Fast-Paced World

Use your struggles to grow stronger.

What can you remember about your childhood? What were the fun activities you were involved in? How did you keep yourself occupied?

Who were your friends? Did you have any special friends? What made these friendships so special?

I remember we climbed trees, created our own indoor and outdoor games, rode our bicycles—without helmets—to the local park. We played on the variety of playground equipment available—jungle gyms, seesaws, swings, roundabouts—and caught tadpoles in the stream running through the park, all without any adult supervision.

We walked or rode to school without adult supervision, and caught public transport, even in the evenings, without adult supervision.

We jumped into a teacher's car, or another parent's car if we were going to a sports match without any need of permission slips signed by our parents.

We listened to the Top 20 hits of the week on a Sunday night from Radio Lourenço Marques (I was raised in Cape Town) on a transistor radio; we watched the international sports teams practicing, and mingled with the players before and after matches, with no security guards evident.

We listened to the radio, as we did not have television—Kit Grayson Rides the Range, or something like that, was the daily weekday special at about 5.00 pm; Pick-a-Box, a weekly quiz show; Squad Cars, a detective program; Mark Saxon or something similar . . . yes, those were the days and how different from life today.

The rare computers were massive machines in large office areas with punch cards . . . and so I could go on.

These thoughts occurred after I read an interesting blog by occupational therapist and psychotherapist Victoria Prooday, *The Silent Tragedy Affecting Today's Children*[1], which has been read by over thirty million people since it was published.

Victoria expresses concern about the alarming statistics released by researchers over a fifteen-year period during the early years of this century—for example, one in five children with mental health problems; a 43 percent increase in ADHD; a 37 percent increase in teen depression, and a 200 percent increase in suicide rates in children aged between 10 and 14 years old.

An article in *The Australian* newspaper a while ago quoted Michael Carr-Gregg, a leading Australian psychologist, pointing out that one in every seven students in primary school, and one in four in secondary schools had suffered mental health issues, while youth suicide in Australia was at its worst in ten years.

"This is a generation that is really struggling: I've never seen anything like it," Michael said. "It speaks to me of a lack of resilience. The bottom line is that I don't think we are preparing even the little kids or the biggest kids for adversity."

Both Victoria and Michael express concerns about questionable parenting practices, while I have seen more and more drone parenting (yes, it's that bad!) in recent years.

Clearly, we could be raising a generation that might struggle a great deal in the years ahead, all the more so if 50 percent of the current jobs will no longer exist, as some researchers are suggesting.

If we don't encourage our children to be creative and innovative, to climb trees and even fall out of them at times, to fail while trying something new, to verbally fight their own battles, what can we expect?

Researchers Karen Reivich and Andrew Shatte state that:

---

1. Prooday, *The Silent Tragedy*.

... beliefs can be changed and abilities can be boosted ... Our work on the nature of resilience shows that it is comprised of seven abilities: emotion regulation, impulse control, empathy, optimism, causal analysis, self-efficacy, and reaching out. These seven concrete factors can be measured, taught, and improved.[2]

There are ongoing issues around teenagers not having sufficient sleep, having poor diets, not exercising enough, if at all, spending too much time being negatively impacted by social media instead of "talking" to their friends, and there are increasing anxiety issues, just to mention a few examples.

Bullying in a variety of forms rears its ugly head—cyber bullying an ongoing issue—and parents, teachers, and students require understanding of how to approach bullying and so-called bullying issues.

This is where promoting the spirit of mentoring can play such a critical role in the life of adolescents, as those teenagers (and young adults) communicate with significant adults in their lives who might not be their parents.

While there are justifiable concerns about the protection and bubble-wrapping of our young people, it is relatively easy to change the narrative, and develop strategies for self-empowering our youth.

As a mentor, I can ask some non-threatening questions, listen to the answers, and make some suggestions before we collaboratively develop strategies to live lives that might positively impact our community.

My mentees can work out their personal best goals, take ownership of them, and invite me to join them on the journey for a season or two—for as long as that young person wishes me to take on that encouraging and supportive role.

Here are a few thoughts from my book, *The Spirit of Mentoring—a manual for adult volunteers*.[3]

They are simply examples of possible ways to create positive discussions with a view to assisting your mentee to live a healthy and balanced life, which I have successfully used over the years.

- How have you been doing in your schoolwork during the past three months? Compare your results. What are your strong and weak

---

2. Reivich and Shatte, *The Resilience Factor*, 33.
3. Cox, *The Spirit of Mentoring*.

subjects? What subjects do you enjoy? Why? What subjects don't you enjoy? Why not? What can we do to improve things for you?

- So, you think your schoolwork isn't great and you want to leave school? Have you thought about the importance of gaining the best education you possibly can to help your long-term career prospects? Let's share some ideas.

- How much homework or extra study do you have? How are you handling it? Are there any ways I can support you, or are there any resources you need?

- How much sleep do you get at night? When do you concentrate best in class, at work, or during your training (as applicable)?

- How important are your friendships? Are your friends having a positive or negative influence on your life?

- Do you feel at times that your life is an emotional roller-coaster out of control? That is normal at your age. Would you like me to share what adolescent brain research is suggesting to put you at ease?

- Let's look at the way you spend your time each week. I'll share how I manage my time if you would like me to.

- What career or careers are you interested in? Let's spend part of the mentoring journey exploring some of these options, and see how much information you can find out about these careers. What subjects do you need to study for this career? Where can you further your studies? What are the opportunities for a job in this area? Maybe I can introduce you to friends who are in a career that you are interested in finding out more about. What are the options?

- What really interests you? What are you good at?

- Do you have a part-time job? What is it like? How many hours each week are you working? What do you like or not like about it? Are you saving any money? Should we discuss how to budget?

- If you were applying for a part-time job, you might need a resume. Would you like me to help you draw up a resume?

- Your examinations start in three weeks. Let's draw up a realistic revision schedule together.

- Are you eating a regular breakfast? What are you having? And, what are you having for lunch?

- How much time are you spending on social media each day and night? Would you like me to share some tips about the responsible use of social media?
- How much exercise are you having each week?
- Are you using a diary? I am happy to show you my diary, and we can explore ways of managing your time better so you will end up having more free time.
- Are there any particular sports you enjoy? Tell me about them. Have you been to any matches? Would you like to try out a sport?
- Imagine you have only two years left on earth. What do you want to achieve by the end of that time so that people will appreciate the difference you have tried to make? (This often leads to the discovery of a young person's passion.)

Sowing the seeds of the spirit of mentoring powerfully speaks messages of *hope* and possibility into the lives of our young people.

If we can create partnerships with parents and teachers, as well as employers (where relevant), we shall raise a generation of resilient young people ready to face the challenges of the twenty-first century, and to create all those new jobs we do not even know about yet.

> But resilience isn't just the ability to persevere. . . . it is also an outlook we can cultivate to stay focused on the important things in life rather than what is most urgent, and to keep ourselves from being carried away by negative emotions.
> —Hector Garcia and Francesc Miralles[4]

Perhaps there is no more important time than today to invest time in the lives of our young people.

Who is the young person to whom you can reach out today?

---

4. Garcia and Miralles, *Ikigai*.

WEEK 7

'How Do I Know That You are Genuine? Can You Be Trusted?'

Give your best effort to everything you do.

How many times has someone betrayed the trust you shared with them? How has this affected your relationships? How easy do you find it to trust others?

There are a handful of people I trust, and they are mostly family members.

Most of us have probably been let down by people we trusted. Of course, there were times when we were growing up in school environments, and enjoyed fluctuating friendships. I shared something more personal with a friend, the friendship went sour, and suddenly it felt like the world knew all about what I had shared with that friend.

It is easy to find fault in others, though the deeper questions might be, "How do I know you are genuine? Can you be trusted?"

SEVEN STRATEGIES TO BUILD TRUST

While we strive to become a positive person of influence, we can continually work at building trust with those with whom we communicate. Here are seven simple strategies gathered from my research over the years.

1. *Be authentic.* Be true to your unique personality, values, and spirit at *all* times. Others see you, for example, as credible, legitimate, and authoritative—able to be trusted as being accurate, reliable, and true.

2. *Display empathy.* Do your best to try and understand how a person is feeling, what and why they are thinking this or that; be non-judgmental—walk in their shoes for a while as best as you can, and sometimes feel the blisters.

3. *Be present.* Make yourself open to others by being tuned into your relationship environment. People want to connect, and will do so when you are *transparent*—remember: "We're all in this together."

4. *Tell people where they stand.* People need to know where they stand so they can let go of their fears and questions like: "Am I good enough?" "Do I belong?" When you let people know where they stand, this builds and strengthens positive and meaningful *relationships*.

5. *Provide context in every interaction.* A picture with a frame becomes a different picture. Without background, fear can be elevated by confusion and uncertainty. Providing context moves people from uncertainty to understanding.

6. *Be a catalyst co-creating in conversations.* Frame conversations as dialogues rather than monologues, so people's voices are heard. Create higher levels of engagement and co-creation so people can build a picture of *shared success*—growing people, and further empowering them.

7. *Use honesty at all times.* Tell the *truth*—tactfully, and within the appropriate context.

I spent a year mentoring a younger colleague, Leilani, who was struggling in a number of areas. She approached me, but first we had to build that trust. I was guided by these seven strategies. At the end of the year, Leilani sent me this note:

> I can't thank you enough for all the HOPE you have instilled in me this year. You never once let me give up, and constantly reminded me of my passion and why I started this journey. I never once doubted your wise words, but often found myself using and copying them—they just made sense!

How about you? Any further thoughts from your experiences?

WEEK 8

Life Skills—Be Coachable

Make your choices carefully, for each decision is a part of your destiny.

When you look in the mirror, who do you see? Do you love the person you see?

How well do you deal with conflict? Do you see conflict as a positive or a negative in your personal growth?

Are you a good team player? Do you want people you lead or influence to surpass you?

How easy do you find it to affirm people? How many times do you offer a smile or a gentle, helping hand to someone, especially when you are in a hurry?

When I was a school principal, I undertook a personal challenge for one month. I shared the challenge with my colleagues in the school leadership team.

I asked them to look out for moments to thank our colleagues for a job well done, or a time when they had helped someone, or just been a positive person of influence. All I wanted was for them to share their observation with me. My focus was on *everyone* who contributed to the community in any way: the ground staff, the cleaners, the kitchen staff, the administrative staff, and the teachers.

Each time I observed something, I wrote a brief hand-written (not typed) note to the person thanking them for their effort. Over the month, all colleagues received a note, including members of my senior leadership team. The positive vibe around the school was noticeable.

Of course, this was not the only time I thanked colleagues for their efforts, but I wanted to share with others what happens when we work as a team and look for the positive qualities of others.

Some time ago, I read an article that highlighted ten skills, collated from feedback from chief human resources and strategy officers from leadership global employees responding to questions about the top skills required for the workplace in the future.

They make for interesting reading, and are certainly challenging, especially during these post-pandemic times.

Many of these skills suggest the power of teamwork, looking to become a positive person of influence, and modeling an essential quality—often missing in many workplaces and other interpersonal interactions—*empathy*. When we do our best to walk in the shoes of others, we can impact lives in significant ways.

Reflect on these skills and how you feel you measure up.

1. Complex problem solving.
2. Critical thinking.
3. Creativity.
4. People management.
5. Coordinating with others.
6. Emotional intelligence.
7. Judgments and decision making.
8. Service orientation.
9. Negotiation.
10. Cognitive flexibility, or the ability to switch between thinking about two different concepts, or to think about multiple concepts simultaneously.

I have served under a variety of leaders, some of whom have been superb, others fairly average. I myself have also held different leadership positions over the years.

Whether it's looking in the mirror at my own leadership efforts, or thinking about those who have led me, I can confidently state that none of us can claim to have mastered all ten of these suggested skills.

How coachable are you?

One school principal I worked under told me that, if at least five of the staff had not been promoted to senior management positions in other schools by the end of a year, he felt he had failed in his role as a school principal. A wonderful message of encouraging others to reach their God-given potential, which I never forgot.

There are those magical moments when we visualize for a person something about their gifts and talents which, for whatever reason, they might not be seeing—a powerful mentoring, potentially life-changing moment.

Which of the above skills can you chat about with your mentee when you next meet?

WEEK 9

10 Life Lessons for a Purposeful Life

Be focused on personal growth, and always practice gratitude.

When you were a teenager, did you ever feel that your life had no purpose? Maybe you were drifting? Did you feel pressure to conform to peers, or to feel that you belonged?

Did you have bold dreams, yet were afraid to chase them—why was this?

Did you risk failure to achieve something special? Did you allow either positive or negative friends to influence you the most?

Did you have to overcome some obstacle, illness, or other setback?

Mark, a talented sportsman; Brittany, revealing signs of antisocial behavior; Ollie, disengaging from school; Holly, feeling overwhelmed with life's challenges, and Mia, facing the real prospect of failing, were young people I worked with over a period of time, encouraging them to strive to reach their potential.

Each one of them made significant choices and now, some years later, to the best of my knowledge, they are all achieving great things because each of them followed the majority of the *10 Habits to Become the Best You can Be,* which guided them to develop lives with meaning and purpose.

The idea of framing a teenager's life around these ten habits was developed over many years of coaching and mentoring young people.

These habits provide an achievable set of guidelines or targets to share with a teenager, and also build resilience.

> Resilient people know how to stay focused on their objectives, on what matters, without giving in to discouragement. Their flexibility is the source of their strength. They know how to adapt to change and to reversals of fortune. They concentrate on the things they can control and don't worry about those they can't.
> —Hector Garcia and Francesc Miralles[1]

When a young person feels unconditionally cared for, that their opinions are heard and valued, and they begin to see some meaning and purpose in their lives, they are on the way to fulfilling their potential.

10 HABITS TO BECOME THE BEST YOU CAN BE

The *10 Habits to Become the Best You can Be* offers young people important choices.

When they have a significant adult walking alongside them, as they choose their future pathway, more often than not you will witness significant, positive developments occurring, as well as the emergence of a more resilient person able to bounce back in challenging times.

1. Surround myself with *positive friends* and be a positive person of influence; become a great listener, respecting the viewpoints of others, and a team player who prides myself on the responsible use of social media.
2. Follow a *hobby or interest* during the next thirty days. Listen to music; study art or photography; take up reading; dance, skateboard, try a new sport, create, or develop something new . . . broaden my interests; show a spirit of curiosity and inquiry.
3. *Exercise* at least thirty minutes every second day—*at least* 2.5 hours a week. Exercise is exceptionally good for my positive brain development.
4. Spend at least ten minutes a day quietly *reflecting* on my life and purpose as I follow my passion/s. Get in touch with my feelings—own them.

---

1. Garcia and Miralles, *Ikigai*.

5. Have at least *nine hours of sleep* every night, as sleep enables the brain to consolidate memory and learning, benefits my diet, and also helps me to manage my stress better.

6. Join a *youth, cultural, or community club,* to learn how to appreciate, respect and tolerate different people and cultures.

7. Look for *three adults I trust* with my life (in addition to my parents), and stay in touch with them as they become my wise guides on the side, my non-judgmental cheerleaders.

8. Give priority in my life to my *school subjects, tertiary study program, or work (career journey)*, seeking to be innovative, entrepreneurial and creative, unafraid to step out of my comfort zone; willing to learn from those who have travelled before me—read history and great novels to improve my understanding of different thinkers and cultures; develop a strong work ethic.

9. Set myself specific, measurable, intentional, extending (taking me out of my comfort zone), realistic *goals* that I know I can achieve. Use short and small action steps as I chase my dreams, supported by my cheerleaders.

10. *Be myself.* I am unique. I can have fun. I will do nothing life-threatening; aware that it is okay to risk failure as those experiences are an important part of my self-discovery and self-learning journey.

Lauren, a 10-year-old student, offers some wise words: "Believing is a word that means thinking you can. If you fail to succeed, try, try again. Achieving is a word that means reaching your goal. But you must believe and look deep in your soul."

When you move alongside a teenager for a season of their lives, spend time getting to know them, and what they are thinking. As you do this and reveal an empathetic and non-judgmental attitude, they will open the door of trust, and allow you into their lives.

This will happen in different ways and at different times, dependent on the life journey of the individual with whom you are communicating.

Sometimes, no matter how hard you try, obstacles come in the way of your relationship with your mentee. Perhaps you have felt totally helpless when you tried to assist someone struggling with personal issues to move into a better head space?

This was my experience with Max, as I'll explain in a

I know I cannot be a savior, nor a rescuer, and my teaching, mentoring, or coaching role is not about "fixing" families or people.

I have found over the years that working with adolescents is considerably more challenging when the family is not functioning well.

I have seen "drone parents" getting in the way, and protecting their children because they have their own agendas for their children. These parents contribute to the emergence of a "powderpuff" generation of young people who will struggle in an increasingly entrepreneurial, innovative world where one might have to risk failure to achieve dreams.

I have seen parents with their own mental health issues become a mixture of drone, or helicopter parents. They hover and interfere, and much depends on their own mood swings with regard to how they react to situations involving their children.

Wearing my education and mentoring hats, as well as reflecting on years of experience working with young people, I can see the potential damage a parent's suffocating love can cause.

I try and sow positive seeds of *hope*, trusting that one day the young person will remember the discussions, find a mentor, and start putting into action some of their own ideas without fearing failure, or trying to be perfect.

While talking with sixteen-year-old Max, we discussed the ten habits mentioned above, initially focusing on

- goals—how to set personal best goals; why goals can help one find meaning and purpose; why it is important to write the goals down and take ownership of them;
- choices—the choices we make will define our future. Sometimes, due to circumstances, we might not be able to make the choice we would like. At this point we need to learn how we choose to adapt to a different life situation;
- how to develop significant relationships—we talked about positive and negative peer pressure, as well as the characteristics and values we appreciate in friends;
- self-image and developing high self-esteem—I wove thoughts about these matters into all our conversations;

- values—we shared thoughts on respect for oneself and others, integrity, tolerance, gratitude, compassion, empathy, and other values relevant to the discussion at the time;
- careers—we explored possible career pathways, and explored Max's passions in life.

Max was enthusiastic, and headed off to take up some of the challenges. Sadly, he lacked the determination to tackle the personal best goals he set for himself.

His mother always made excuses and Max, as a normal and often confused teenager, took advantage of that situation. He did not appear to understand that he was falling further and further behind his peers.

When it was clear that Max was not reacting positively to all the support he was receiving, and making excuse after excuse for not delivering academic projects on time, his mother moved him to another school, his third school in as many years.

Often, I have seen how absent, or inadequate, or incompetent parenting has resulted in the adolescent's antisocial behavior escalating. Brain research tells us that this can ultimately lead to delinquency, and chronic criminal behavior.

Brain researchers also suggest that severe and chronic stress in an adolescent's life can also be linked to physical and emotional abuse, though the good news is that deficits might not be permanent because of the plasticity of the brain.

Whenever I have worked with adolescents in these challenging situations, I have *always* consulted people more experienced than I am with regard to mental health issues. I inevitably receive encouragement, and some helpful tips to keep on keeping on.

Just being present for a young person, and sharing a thought or an idea, might be a life-changing moment I only hear about years later, or maybe never hear about.

Author Robert Louis Stevenson left us with an appropriate challenge: "Don't judge each day by the harvest you reap, but by the seeds you plant."

Have you ever had a similar experience you can share with others?

WEEK 10

Five Proven Key Qualities of a Great Mentor

Character is more important than reputation.

Do you think young people, especially teenagers, need volunteer adult mentors to guide them through the challenging years of their adolescence?

I was close to completing my daily morning walk as I passed two groups of students on their way to school. The first group was about thirteen years of age, boys trying to grab the attention of the girls, nothing unusual about that. The second group was a year or two older, and this time two girls were trying to attract the attention of three or four boys.

Listening to the banter going on between these young people, the impact that peer pressure was having on each of them, probably in different ways, underlined for me how important it is for young people to have non-judgmental, trusted adult cheerleaders in their lives.

Clearly, these two groups of students valued a connection with peers, that sense of belonging. How that plays out during the day, weeks, and months, I have no idea, though some relationships will probably be strengthened, and others might become wobbly, even fall apart.

Who do these young people turn to for encouragement, support and guidance, I wondered?

Well-known author, Ted Engstrom, shared these thoughts in an article I read some time ago:

> What kind of mentor impacts the world? I think it would be a person of *vision* who has the ability to see potential in his mentee, a person not intimidated by difficulties . . . a person with *commitment* to go the distance and make a difference in the life of another . . . a person who gives *priority* to the Kingdom of God and His righteousness . . . one who understands *accountability*, and one whose life is open to a few trusted confidants and who demands of mentees the same appraisal.

I remain incredibly grateful to the former school principal who mentored me during my final couple of years as an assistant head—before I retired—someone not associated with the school in any way, a confidant, and wonderful encourager.

Philosopher and educator Herman Horne stated that a mentor has a good heart which implies qualities such as "good humor, charitableness, candor, sympathy, earnestness, empathy, sincerity, and modesty." The good conversationalist, he goes on to say, is one who can not only talk, but also *listen* well.

FIVE KEY QUALITIES OF A GREAT MENTOR

Author, Bob Biehl, in his superb book, *Mentoring*[1], shared five key qualities of a great mentor, which contain some helpful mentoring tips. I have made additional comments in some places.

1. *Love:* Love or care for your mentee . . . express that love with care—for example, using expressions like, "I feel some of what you are feeling." "I care that you are hurting." "I care that you are struggling right now." When this unconditional care is expressed, it creates life-changing moments in the lives of mentees, especially teenagers.

2. *Encourage:* As a good mentor, be an encourager, affirmer, recognizer and cheerleader. Be the person in your mentee's life that keeps giving them the message: "You are going to make it, and I'll be with you every step of the way, or for as long as you want me to walk alongside you."

---

1. Biehl, *Mentoring*.

FIVE PROVEN KEY QUALITIES OF A GREAT MENTOR

3. *Be open*: Share with your mentees. Tell them about your failures as well as your successes. Young people, especially, love to hear true stories which can inspire and motivate them to have the courage to step out of their comfort zone and start chasing dreams.

4. *Check your motives:* Your role is to build up your mentee, to nurture, guide, encourage, and support. *Never* use the mentee for your own purposes.

5. *Relax*: Young people want mentors. Be comfortable in the relationship. Care for them and, when you meet, simply ask two mentoring questions: "What are your priorities?" and "How can I help you?" Then relax, have plenty of fun, keep a sense of humor, and enjoy the relationship.

These are wise words, and a reminder how special all volunteer mentors are when they step up to guide others and, most especially, follow one of the golden rules of mentoring: "*Never* quit on them!"

Then there is that memorable moment when your mentoring season draws to a close, and you reflect on your time together.

Fourteen-year-old Amelia became sick with an illness that doctors took a while to diagnose. She loved school, and was actively involved in many activities. She became too sick to attend school, yet wanted to keep studying when she felt stronger. There were times she was able to return to school for a while, and then had to step back and rest.

I mentored Amelia for three years, during which time I kept in touch with her through the school's secure email system. On her final day at school, she presented me with a card in which she wrote:

> Thank you for being such an incredible supporter and guide over the past three years. Your constant help and faith have strengthened me and given me hope an innumerable number of times. Thank you for always believing in me, praying for me, supporting me, and guiding me to God's love. You've impacted my life in a very positive way and I can't thank you enough for that.

Thankfully, Amelia recovered from her illness, gained a university degree, and, when last I heard, she was happily married and holding a management position in a company.

Whose life are you investing your time and energy in at the moment?

WEEK 11

'You Have the Seeds of Greatness Within You.' A Helpful Perspective

Be willing to strike out. It's the only way to greatness.

> First say to yourself what you would be; and then do what you have to do.
> —Epictetus
>
> People are always blaming their circumstances for what they are. I don't believe in circumstances. The people who get on in this world are the people who get up and look for the circumstances they want, and, if they can't find them, they make them.
> —George Bernard Shaw

Read through those two quotes a couple of times and think about your response to them.

There is a strong message here about the way we choose our future pathways, and the words we use when we share thoughts and ideas with mentees.

In discussions I have had with teenagers over the years, there have been many students who made excuses for not reaching their potential, especially when they did something wrong, and were found out.

Some of the more popular comments would be:

- "It's my parents' fault. They're always fighting. Life at home sucks."
- Or maybe a parent has an addiction of some sort which makes life at home tough.
- Or they want to keep their circle of friends. These friends keep breaking rules, but being with those friends is more important than reaching their potential. Negative peer pressure tends to lead to negative behavior. We drag ourselves down. Why?
- "It's the teacher's fault. He (or she) doesn't like me."
- Or, one of the classic comments: "I didn't think about the consequences of my actions." (Brain research tells us that this can be a genuine situation, as the prefrontal cortex, the chief executive area of the brain, where decision-making is taking place, is still developing until the mid-twenties.)

Instead of standing on their own two feet and learning how to take responsibility for their choices and behavior, they prefer to blame everyone else. In the defense of some students, they might have no idea how to seek assistance before they make choices. The *blame mentality* is not the way to move forward.

The situation has increasing challenges, as more and more young people live in a world of instant gratification and entitlement. Or, to put it another way, author and retired pastor John Cox writes:

> We probably all remember the excuses that bounced from our lips like popcorn: "I'm tired . . . I'll do it later . . . I don't feel like it . . . Something else came up . . . It wasn't what I expected . . ." and so on. There is always a moment when we hit the proverbial wall. We can either press on without the initial passion we once had for the project, or we can stop altogether and bear the consequences.[1]

Holocaust survivor, Viktor Frankel, offers some sage advice: "Everything can be taken from a man or woman but one thing: the last of human freedoms—to choose one's attitude in any given set of circumstances, to choose one's own way."

No matter what the situation might be, I have the ability to make my choices about how to respond to what's going on around me; to appreciate that there are no quick-fix solutions or easy answers to the challenges I face in life.

1. Cox, *99 Musings*, 209.

There are positive messages anyone working with young people can weave into their conversations. Eventually that young person might take ownership of their thoughts and feelings, especially when they have a non-judgmental adult *of their choice* walking alongside and guiding them: "You have the seeds of greatness within you. You can be a positive influence. You can make a difference."

I recall sixteen-year-old Scarlett's journey, having been through significantly challenging family circumstances. She was determined to reach her full potential, and valued the support given to her. When she finished her schooling, she sent me this note:

> Thank you for always believing in me and encouraging me to set higher standards for myself, striving further to reach my ambitions. You have had a profound impact in my life, and I am so grateful for all the lessons you've taught me (or guided me to).

Scarlett enjoyed an outstanding university career, and is now a company manager chasing her dreams.

Each of us has the seeds of greatness within us, or the ability to reach our God-given potential. I make my choice and start heading in that direction, others might observe me, and want to be like me. They start asking me questions, and commenting that I have changed.

As I share my story, I make a positive difference in the lives of those around me, which is a humbling experience.

One of the major shifts in my thinking takes place when I can look in the mirror and honestly state: "I am lovable, and I am capable."

This is true of each and every one of us. It was certainly true of Scarlett.

The major goal we can continually strive to achieve is to *be myself*.

One of my key life philosophies is: *Life is a learning experience*.

As long as you are willing to learn, you will go *far*.

WEEK 12

Boys Will be Boys! Embracing the Individuality of Young Minds

Be of service to others, and kind to everyone you meet.

Can you remember the teacher who brought out the best work, or kept you most interested and motivated in school and schoolwork?

This is a great question to ask your mentee, or any adolescent you are working with. Their response will provide you with insights into how they are developing.

When I was eight years old my class teacher had a significant impact on my life. Miss Wolfe was tough, thorough, kind and compassionate, and set clear boundaries. She was not interested in a second-rate effort, and expected all her students to do their best. I did well academically in those days and learnt, at this young age, how to study and prepare for tests, whilst also having plenty of fun in the classroom. Miss Wolfe had a beautiful Alsatian dog, Alannah, which she occasionally brought to school—yes, this was allowed in those days. We all loved Alannah.

There were other teachers during my primary or junior school years who kept me interested in school work, but Miss Wolfe was special.

When I underwent cancer operations, even though I had moved up the school, Miss Wolfe monitored my progress, wrote me a letter wishing me a speedy recovery, and kindly gave me a book of animals which I kept for about fifty years until it fell apart.

Miss Wolfe's attitude, care and compassion, had a significant impact on my decision to become a teacher.

During my last couple of years of schooling Dave Hiscock, my history teacher, had a significant impact on my education journey.

Dave's teaching methods were far ahead of his time. We researched topics, exploring and considering different viewpoints, and then discussed our findings as a class. There was no regurgitation of information, no political correctness, or fear of discussing the heresy of apartheid—I grew up in South Africa—rather the importance of having an open mind, and looking at all topics objectively. In a way we were taught the importance of being independent learners.

Then there was the day that Dave passed me in the school grounds and warned me, in his typically forthright, no-nonsense manner, that if I didn't knuckle down to produce some consistent work, I could well fail history in my final year of school. Too much sport, not enough focus on my academic studies, and Dave called it as he saw it.

My response? I took up the challenge. My history result was my best result in my final year, and I went on to major in history at university, became a history teacher, and was mentored by Dave for a number of years during the early stages of my teaching career.

My reflections reminded me of two interesting books I read a while ago, both having a specific focus on boys. *The Trouble with Boys* by Peg Tyre, and *Reaching Boys, Teaching Boys—Strategies that Work and Why* by Michael Reichert and Richard Hawley.

While the emphasis of these books was on how boys are being educated within a school environment, there were many comments made by the authors that underline key aspects of the spirit of mentoring.

Peg Tyre quoted psychologist Michael Reichert, ". . . boys base their behavior not on what we say we want them to do but on what we do ourselves as men, the kind of behavior that is modeled for them by authority figures. The kind of behavior that is ratified and held up for praise in their community."[1]

An interesting question to ask a mentee: "What are you being taught at school about how to think and how to behave as men?"

---

1. Tyre, *The Trouble with Boys*.

Much research states that boys want to be respected rather than liked. The authors of these books reiterate that what works with boys is baseline rigor, respect, and mutual trust.

What do these qualities look like in an adolescent boy's life? They could include, not in any particular order:

- the effective use of a diary;
- learning how to get organized, and stay organized;
- spending no more than two hours a day on gaming (though more recently researchers are suggesting less time per day);
- developing good graphomotor skills—the skills needed for writing to take place—so they can clearly express their ideas;
- a variety of activities and structure—clear rules and directions;
- the involvement of dads;
- linking the relevance of what they are learning to their lives;
- never humiliating them in public;
- good sleep (nine hours every night) and a healthy diet;
- scaffolding them while they try something and fail, so they can rebound and try again;
- acknowledging and recognizing them, especially their *efforts*—a quiet gesture, or a great fanfare in front of their peers when they succeed (always mindful of being culturally appropriate);
- encouraging connections with mentors, caring teachers, or other significant adults;
- relational teaching—where boys are known beyond a seating chart, a test score, or a semester grade;
- lessons that address something deep and personal in their lives: their sexuality, their character, their personal prospects in the world beyond school—novelty, drama, surprise, active learning, movement, teamwork, competition, and risk taking.

Reichert and Hawley suggest that "where boys were emotionally and intellectually engaged by their teachers, they convey a sense of being transported, exploring new territory, and feeling newly effective, interested and powerful."[2]

2. Reichert and Hawley, *Reaching Boys*.

The authors remind their readers that the brains of these young men are still developing, and we must be mindful of this when we are assessing their progress or lack of progress. We can show an understanding that most fourteen-and fifteen-year-old boys are unable to make judgments like adults. Their prefrontal cortex area of the brain is still developing, and they reach cognitive efficiency later in life when compared to girls.

Peg Tyre reminds readers that "often a boy's gruff exterior is masking confusion and fear—boys desperately need connections with each other and with adults,"[3] hence the importance of boys having constructive relationships with well-meaning, non-judgmental mentors who can journey with them on their path to manhood.

Reichert and Hawley quote a senior school student who shared the impact a positive teacher had on his adolescent journey: "She never gave up on me, even though I kept on having difficulty, and finally, after many morning and lunch extra help sessions, a light finally turned on in my mind and I understood everything . . . she never gave up on me and always believed that I could do it . . . she went the extra mile to help me, and that's what makes this school so great."[4]

Many boys—indeed, many adolescents—think the adult world is not listening, and not generally interested in their views, their well-being, their educational needs, and outcomes.

The mentoring relationship allows a significant adult to step into a young man's life, *genuinely* welcoming him as a person with gifts and talents to be nurtured and encouraged.

The mentor displays warmth, humor, passion and care, and is always fair.

The mentor uses the time with their mentee to share personal stories which might inspire and motivate the mentee to chase his dream, and reach his potential.

As a mentor, how would you respond to three questions your mentee might ask you:

1. Do you know me?

2. Are you interested in me?

3. How does my life matter to you?

3. Tyre, *The Trouble with Boys*.
4. Reichert and Hawley, *Reaching Boys*.

WEEK 13

'I am Tired of Living Like This. Please Help.' Mila's Story

Be willing to light another's candle.

How do you respond when someone walks into your life and asks you to help them?

This was my experience with Mila.

Mila was in her final year of school and was one of the top students academically.

A couple of weeks before Mila approached me, I had delivered a presentation to all the final year students and their parents, sharing thoughts and strategies on how to cope with the year ahead.

After my talk, Mila's mum spoke to me and thanked me for all I had shared. She suggested to Mila that she ask me to help her plan her final year.

Mila talked to me as she felt she needed some assistance to lead a more balanced and healthier lifestyle.

Mila's parents were successful professionals in their respective fields, and Mila commented how much she wanted to please them, which had added to the pressures she was under.

The previous year Mila had obtained superb academic results, and was starting to feel the pressure to achieve these results again.

She told me that, even though she had done really well, these results had come at a great personal cost. The stress had negatively impacted her health.

"I am tired of living like this. Please can you help me?"

"How many hours sleep a night are you having?" I asked.

"Probably about five during the pressure times."

"Well, therein could lie one problem," I suggested, "so let's focus on the organization of your time and how you plan, with at least nine hours sleep *every* night becoming a habit."

THE TEENAGE BRAIN NEEDS SLEEP

I remain continually puzzled that many parents seem reluctant to ensure that their teenage children have a minimum of nine hours sleep every night. More and more research points to the necessity of this, as puberty is kicking in, and the brain is at an important stage of its developmental journey.

The brain needs sleep to regulate emotions, to dispose of unimportant information, lay down new learning, and to process new information.

Basically, the brain needs sleep to grow, change, and re-energize so it can function properly during the following day. Scientists have learned that what our brain learns during the day is consolidated during sleep.

Author and brain researcher, Nicola Morgan[1], says there is more and more evidence now suggesting that our sleeping brains practice the things we do while we are awake.

Nicola describes how REM sleep (Rapid Eye Movement sleep), during which time our eyelids are fluttering, happens at certain stages during the sleep cycle, particularly when we are experiencing deep sleep and dreaming. Research is now suggesting that REM sleep is particularly important for memory and learning.

During adolescence changes to the brain affect the biological clock, a cluster of neurons that sends signals throughout the body, and control all the internal operations, one of which is sleep.

Melatonin, the chemical that is released to induce sleep, is produced about three hours later in the 24-hour sleep cycle of teenagers compared to adults and younger children. The teenager, who strives to be more independent, and tries to control their life—possibly working late because of questionable management of time issues—has a problem.

1. Morgan, *Blame My Brain*.

Again, when we discuss all this with them—and most teenagers find the topic fascinating—and work out a new management of time plan, all will be well.

There will be times when teenagers do work late and get up early for school and, come the weekend, they might want to sleep for a long time. This is normal—let them do so.

ENCOURAGING AND MOTIVATING MILA

Let's get back to Mila's story.

I agreed to help Mila on condition that she understood that our conversations would actually be geared towards preparing her for university the following year. She agreed to this.

The message I often shared with Mila was that every day when she awoke to begin a new day, she was responsible for the choices she made. Every choice has a consequence. We unpacked the meaning of this regularly.

As we prepared to share thoughts and ideas, Mila spoke of her academic, sporting, cultural, and student leadership goals for the rest of the year.

I began with focusing on sleep patterns, and management of time, encouraging Mila to explore different options until she found strategies to give her the best chance of reaching her full potential. Within a couple of weeks, she had moved to a place of having nine hours sleep a night, and was already noticing the difference.

She had also started an exercise program, and was reporting that she felt less stressed, and happier as a person.

Not only is a consistent sleep pattern desired, but proper nutrition also enhances the developing brain. Psychologist Andrew Fuller has done a lot of work in this area over many years. Andrew's work supports other research which suggests that, where we pay attention to nutrition and cognition, memory, attention, stress and intelligence, there is a greater possibility of positive student achievement.

I have had numerous conversations with students about the importance of eating a healthy breakfast, so that they can stay sharp and focused during their lessons. Fortunately, this was a strength in Mila's lifestyle, though we monitored her health and well-being throughout the year.

Mila and I had many discussions about the impact of positive and negative peer pressure, and how to effectively manage a busy schedule. She appreciated that, as the year drew to a close and the focus moved to her final exams, she had to cut back on her extracurricular commitments.

I had noticed at a student leadership camp before the beginning of the school year, how Mila arrived, sat down—students were seated in a large circle—and proceeded to silently check out all the other students.

Once I felt Mila and I had connected, and some trust had been created between us, I brought up this event, and simply said: "At the leadership camp I observed how you arrived and sat looking around at all the other students. Were you concerned about how you measured up, and how you were dressed compared to others?"

She acknowledged that was exactly what she was thinking.

And so began many conversations about being oneself, being authentic, choosing one's friends carefully, listening to the opinions of others with respect and empathy, while also having fun.

One day Mila arrived to tell me that she had made some decisions with regard to the friends she intended hanging around with. She had decided that those who were negative would be excluded from her life at school, and she proceeded to action this with positive results.

Mila was a high achiever and terrified of failure, a common challenge to people of all ages. We discussed the importance of taking calculated risks, how to positively interpret failure as a learning curve on life's journey, and how to respond to the question: "What can I take from this experience moving forward?"

Parental pressure did not help, and I was quietly trying to coach Mila how to respond to parental pressure—a helicopter parenting style that was totally unhelpful to her personal growth.

Things came to a head when Mila and a group of friends—positive peer pressure—arranged to meet at the public library to pursue their academic studies. It was also a great social time for them all.

When Mila's parents objected to this, Mila threatened rebellion after her efforts to reason with her parents had stumbled.

I was pleased to see this development in Mila's personal growth occurring. However, I reminded her, that in a few months she would be away from home at university, and able to do whatever she wanted, whenever she wanted. Was it worth the battle with her parents about going to the library? Mila looked at everything through a different lens, and understood that this was a battle not worthy of the effort.

While there were a few ups and downs through the year, Mila worked hard to achieve a healthy and balanced lifestyle. She obtained outstanding results at the end of the year, progressed to university, where she excelled, and is now in her dream profession.

Occasionally she kept in touch with me during her university years. On one occasion it was to seek my encouragement about a relationship issue causing great concern, and on another occasion to share a significant life choice she had made.

The highlight for me was Mila's note she handed to me on her final day at school.

> I cannot thank you enough for your support and guidance this year. Thank you for all of our meetings, they have made a difference to my life and helped me to become a stronger and more resilient person. You have taught me so much about myself and about how to tackle whatever life throws at me. Thank you for listening to my worries and concerns and helping me to transform them into positive areas of growth that I did not even know I was capable of. You have been such a fantastic support system for me and you have set me on the perfect path to take on university and everything else that life has to offer. I will cherish the words I said during one of our meetings, that "It doesn't matter how I get there, as long as I get there," and I will hold onto your many supportive emails over the year . . . I am so grateful that you were a significant part of my final year at school . . .

The spirit of mentoring involves discussions between volunteer adult mentors and their adolescent mentees about effective sleep patterns, effective management of time, setting personal goals, and working out strategies to live healthy and balanced lives. The other life conversations occur as and when the young person desires these.

Have you a story to share about your experiences working in this area with a young person?

WEEK 14

Unlocking Potential: Supporting Teenagers to Set Personal Best Goals

Discover and live your purpose, and create your own path.

What would you do if you could leave school today and had all the qualifications you need? You have to pay rent, transport costs, mobile phone costs, clothing, food and daily living expenses and so on. So, you *must* acquire a job.

That's the type of conversation I often have when I meet teenagers, and develop a meaningful relationship with them.

"I don't know," is an unacceptable answer, as I remind them that they have a good brain that needs to be used.

This conversation inevitably unpacks a passion and, once we have identified that, we talk about future careers, and maybe include an entrepreneurial project while the student is still at school. If the latter, we discuss the possibility of meeting a successful entrepreneur for a further chat. We explore the qualifications needed, skills required, and a university or some other tertiary institution to attend. We share thoughts about living a healthy and balanced lifestyle.

We start identifying strengths, and link these to the goal-getting journey, as this creates a more resilient teenager.

And so, the goal-setting process begins. As the student has meaning and purpose to their life, they appreciate that action is required to achieve this fulfillment of a passion. This conversation becomes the game-changer in many young lives. Suddenly, things begin to clear, and they see a pathway into a bright and potentially exciting future.

15 GOAL-GETTING TIPS AND STRATEGIES FOR EFFECTIVE MENTORS

You can be a parent, or teacher, or coach working alongside a teenager. A parent is likely to have a stronger emotional attachment, so the way this journey plays out might differ slightly from the experience of other significant adults.

These fifteen goal-getting tips and strategies are a collation of my personal mentoring, teaching, and parenting experiences:

1. Make an effort to get to know your mentee before setting goals. Establishing a level of trust and confidentiality enhances the goal-setting process. Understandably, this might not always be possible, in which case tread a little softly until you feel you have a better connection with your mentee.
2. Help your mentee appreciate that they, individually, wield great personal power, as they have control over most of the choices they make.
3. Encourage your mentee to develop a feeling of optimism about their future.
4. Start with easy, specific, achievable, realistic, and measurable seven-day goals—for example, record homework in a diary each day; eat breakfast; get up ten minutes earlier on school days.
5. Receiving feedback on goal achievement is critical for motivation—give it regularly, though make it constructive, and only offer it when your mentee is available to receive it.
6. Often motivation comes, not from the goals themselves, but from feeling dissatisfied if a performance level was not achieved, and wanting to do better next time.
7. Keep revising and revisiting the goals, remaining *flexible*—as lives change, so goals might need to change, especially if new opportunities arise.

8. Look for performance not perfection, and continually look to praise their *efforts*. Let your mentee focus on the question: How do I rate compared to what I see myself capable of becoming?
9. Avoid teasing, nagging, guilt trips—focus on the positive development of your mentee.
10. Give genuine praise, and your mentee will respect your authenticity more than anything else.
11. Look for ways to reward your mentee—behavior that is rewarded tends to be repeated. Devise your own reward scheme such as special certificates, SMS messages, notes, or outings.
12. Encourage your mentee to set goals around the school year—term by term, or semester by semester.
13. Encourage your mentee to use creative ways for setting goals. There is no one method that works for all. Let your mentee experiment and adapt, though they should develop the habit of *writing* down goals, something adolescent brain researchers suggest enhances the development of the brain. Allow for the uniqueness of your mentee.
14. Share some of your own goals with your mentee to show that you are in a partnership, and attempting to build a meaningful relationship.
15. Goals should be aligned with family and cultural values when a mentor is involved in a cross-cultural relationship. The question to ask might be: "What is the attitude of your culture towards education and goal-setting?" Wherever possible, the goals should be shared with the mentee's family.

You might experience some high and low moments during this journey. This is normal. At such times speak to the vision you have of your mentee achieving the goals. Hold on to one of the golden rules of mentoring: "*Never* quit on your mentee."

How and why did you become involved in goal-setting?

Share this story with your mentee.

WEEK 15

How to Help Youth Achieve Personal Best Goals

Focus on growth, and set goals along the way.

What are key ways you can help a young person on the goal-getting journey?

That's the question I asked myself when Glen came to see me. He specifically wanted assistance with planning, organization, and management of his time.

Glen was fortunate, as he was highly motivated, worked hard in and out of the classroom, and had some career goals in place. However, he was feeling stressed, and not sleeping well.

I have learnt over the years that when I encourage a young person to set achievable goals, their lives take on new purpose, and their energies are positively channeled in specific directions.

Indeed, part of the goal-setting process during the mentoring journey is to assist your mentees to make sense of the confusion they may experience (as is normal at this stage of their lives).

TIPS AND STRATEGIES TO SUCCESSFULLY CHASE DREAMS

Here are some tips and strategies which I have adapted and used successfully to help and guide young people to chase their dreams.

- Identify their strengths.
- Identify their passions and interests.
- Determine how they respond to challenges and think about failure. Share legendary basketball player Michael Jordan's experience: "I've missed more than 9000 shots in my career. I've lost almost 300 games. Twenty-six times I've been trusted to take the game winning shot and missed. I've failed over and over again in my life. And that is why I succeed."
- Take non-life-threatening risks in a safe and secure environment.
- Plan, prioritize, and develop strategies using resources available to them.
- Commit to something, and see it through to a conclusion.
- Identify and solve problems; see obstacles as opportunities.
- Evaluate their progress.
- Appreciate that they have control over their choices and goals most of the time.
- Appreciate that a dream is an end in itself, while goals are normally a means to an end—when all the goals (pieces of a puzzle) come together, they realize the dream.
- Guide them how to visualize their personal best goals as if they have already achieved them, thereby increasing their self-confidence and self-esteem.

Also appreciate that:

- you have a role as a coach and a cheerleader, aiming to motivate your mentees to move out of their comfort zone, and become the best they can be;
- your mentees will be looking to their parents, as well as a range of other adults *in loco parentis*—you, teachers, coaches, relatives, workplace superiors—for definitions of life, goals, and values;
- the process of setting personal best goals requires flexible thinking and strategies, patience with your mentees, empathy, perseverance, encouragement, and exemplary modeling.

Glen and I spent about an hour looking at many of the above aspects as I sat in the cheerleader seat that day. He headed off to experiment with some of the strategies we discussed, and returned three weeks' later to share his experiences, at which point we agreed on the best strategies he could follow moving forward.

Glen and I met regularly in the months ahead, and he excelled at school.

How about you?

What obstacles did you face when you set goals during your adolescence? How did you overcome them?

Have you any recent examples of helping a young person on the goal-getting journey?

WEEK 16

The Importance of Patience and Perseverance in Reaching Your Goals

Surround yourself with people who genuinely support you.

> Some people come into our lives and quickly go. Some stay for a while and leave footprints on our hearts. And we are never, ever the same.
> —Author unknown

I love this quote, as it resonates with me and my life journey to date, as I think about all those who have coached, mentored, and encouraged me along the different paths I have travelled.

There have been times when I have been impatient at the lack of progress with an idea, or because other people simply can't catch the vision, while at other times I have wondered what would have happened had I persevered.

How many times can you remember quitting and, as you reflected at a later date, regretted doing so?

Three stories from different past experiences, have shown what perseverance, even patience can mean as individuals strive to achieve different goals.

THE IMPORTANCE OF PATIENCE AND PERSEVERANCE

Australian swimmer Emily Seebohm won the World 200 meters backstroke at the World Championships in Budapest in 2017. From the high standards she had set for herself, she had failed abysmally at the Rio Olympic Games in 2016, and came close to quitting the sport.

Emily was suffering from health issues and, once these were sorted, decided to persevere. Having swum for Australia for many years, few would have begrudged her deciding to retire, as she had won so many medals already.

However, she felt that she had more to achieve, and so began the long, lonely slog of training, and training, and training! Her patience with herself, and her determination not to quit, together with the critical support of key people in her life, helped Emily return to the top of the swimming world in her specialist stroke.

After winning the race at the 2017 World Championships, she made two interesting statements in the post-race interview:

"I was going to be proud of myself whether I won or came last tonight."

"Sometimes you have to go down to go back up."

Emily was striving to be the best swimmer she could be. She trained hard for the World Championships, hence her comment that, no matter what the result might be, she had given it her best shot.

Emily was in that dark, lonely place, and decided, with the support and help of others (a crucial point, and significant in the journey of a mentor and their mentee), she would try once again to keep pushing to become the best she could be.

Emily, now retired, participated in four Olympic Games, won three gold medals, five World Championship medals, and seven Commonwealth Games Gold medals.

While sharing thoughts about champions, another story that caught my eye was that of Australian surfer, Sally Fitzgibbons, winner of four International Surfing Association (ISA) World Titles.

Since 2009 Sally had finished runner-up to the World Champion three times, and was in the top four on three other occasions. What did she say?

"It's [surfing] a way of life that feels insanely good. I just try to make the most of what's in front of me. I wear my heart on my sleeve, and try to compete with that fighting Aussie spirit. You get knocked down and you have to fight and work hard to get back up and keep on charging."

There's the perseverance in play again, though she also said in 2018, "... I am so passionate about my sport and the chance to be a competitor at all. That energizes me every day to get up and go after it. I'm always seeking to learn and become a stronger, more intelligent competitor. After nine years on tour, I now feel nine times stronger, nine times a better surfer, nine times fitter, nine times more experienced, and nine times more intelligent as a competitive surfer."

What drives her? Her passion. What else drives her? A desire to learn. Anything else? She had a goal of becoming the number one surfer in the world, a goal she achieved in June 2019.

My third experience was totally different. I went to see Christopher Nolan's fascinating film, *Dunkirk*, the World War 11 story of the bravery and planning that went into rescuing over 300,000 British and French troops trapped on the beach at Dunkirk in France.

Whether one was in an airplane trying to protect naval and merchant navy ships, or one of a multitude of small boats that journeyed to Dunkirk to rescue these soldiers, or an army officer trying to encourage the troops on the beach, or a soldier having to survive after a ship fetching him was bombed, this was an amazing story of defeating the odds.

The patience of just hanging in and working as a team with fellow soldiers, and the courage of those people who sailed their small boats across the English Channel to rescue the troops on the beach at Dunkirk was inspiring—not giving up in the face of adversity was a real-life message.

The resilience of most of those soldiers meant that they could return to Britain and, in many cases, return to participate in the War.

These are three different true stories that can be shared with mentees, and could lead to discussions around:

- chasing dreams;
- setting goals;
- living a healthy lifestyle;
- working with other trusted people to achieve a goal;
- bouncing back from adversity (resiliency);
- never quitting, and rather learning from every experience;
- moving out of one's comfort zone, and all the risks involved in doing that;
- what it means to strive to become the best one can be;
- identifying strengths, and developing resiliency;

- maybe exploring the life of someone a mentee admires;
- sharing your own story.

Each of our mentees will have their personal story to share. Each will be in a different space. We can take on the mentoring role, and watch our mentee spread their wings and soar positively into the future with our footprint firmly imprinted on their heart.

Emily Seebohm, Sally Fitzgibbons, and all who participated at Dunkirk have stories to share to motivate and inspire each one of us to reach our full potential.

WEEK 17

'Never Quit on Me!' Understand a Teenage Brain

Let go of worry, fear and anxiety, and know that anything is possible.

A rebellious child? Feeling helpless and overwhelmed? Crying out for help to reach and connect with a struggling young person?

This musing might assist that journey.

Do you sometimes struggle to understand what is going on in the world of teenagers? Do you see a beautiful young person one day, and then a monster the next?

Do you tear your hair out at seemingly inexplicable mood swings? Do you throw up your hands in despair? Do you feel you are losing your relationship with a teenager?

Welcome to the normal world of the teenager.

While I was researching adolescent behavior, and the latest adolescent brain research, I jotted down some key aspects of adolescent brain development. This knowledge significantly impacted *how*, when, and why I communicated with teenagers from all walks of life as a parent, teacher, coach, and mentor.

We do well to pause from time to time and remember our own teenage experiences, how we felt at certain times, how we responded to situations and different people as we journeyed through confusing times in search of meaning and purpose in our lives.

Due to the plasticity or malleability of the brain, it can be changed by experiences, a point that should always give *hope* to anyone working with young people.

The frontal lobes make up 40 percent of the brain's total volume. They are the seat of our ability to generate insight, judgment, abstraction, impulse control, and planning. They are the source of self-awareness and our ability to assess dangers and risks, so we use this area of the brain to choose a course of action wisely.

The frontal lobes are said to house the "executive" function of the human brain which only ceases developing in the mid-twenties. So young people need repetition, and to continually learn what responsible choices feel, look, and sound like.

When we are not stressed by negative emotions, we can control what information makes it to our brain. In addition, certain activities like interacting with friends, laughing, participating in physical activities, and acting kindly increase the dopamine (a chemical neurotransmitter) levels in the adolescent brain, which in turn can boost the student's learning, and their ability to process new information.

KEY POINTS FROM ADOLESCENT BRAIN RESEARCH

Here are some of the key points I jotted down as an encouragement to anyone working with teenagers.

- The brain is naturally social and collaborative. When adolescents experience a spirit of belonging, they feel happy, and this adds to their social and emotional well-being.
- Adolescents who believe they have the chance to be successful are intrinsically motivated to learn. The growth of a *positive* mindset is advantageous for the development of the brain.
- Adolescents who are high in self-control do better in school, have higher self-esteem, better, healthier relationships, and fewer problems with anger.
- Scientists reveal that by practicing brain-based skills we can actually change the way our brains look and operate.

- Training and practice will improve skills *and* change our brains, and build its capacity to use these skills.
- Having a growth mindset that encourages adolescents to keep working at these skills will see the development of self-confidence—it's a self-empowering journey.

> Presented with new information, the brain creates new connections and is revitalized. This is why it is so important to expose yourself to change, even if stepping outside your comfort zone means feeling a bit of anxiety.
> —Hector Garcia and Francesc Miralles[1]

- We must provide structures with empowerment in a safe and secure environment to support young people as they find their voices.
- We can encourage a practice of mindfulness on a regular basis, as this helps a young person develop strong coping skills, and resilience in the face of adversity.
- The adolescent brain is only 80 percent of the way to maturity. According to neuroscientist Dr. Francis Jensen[2], the 20 percent gap is where the wiring is thinnest and this helps explain teenage mood swings, irritability, impulsivity, explosiveness, an inability to focus, to follow through, and to connect with adults, and the temptation to use drugs, alcohol, and engage in other risky behavior.
- As the prefrontal cortex is still developing, adolescents struggle to see ahead and understand possible consequences of their choices. They are not fully equipped to weigh up the relative harm of risky behavior. This is why access to positive information and experiences is important (as are interactions with the significant adults in their lives).
- Even though adolescent brains are learning at peak efficiency, much else is inefficient, including attention, self-discipline, task completion, and emotions. In addition, studies of the brain clearly show that reflection inward, or while interacting with others, stimulates the activation and development of the prefrontal cortex towards its integrative growth.

1. Garcia and Miralle, *Ikigai*.
2. Jensen, *The Teenage Brain*.

- Supportive relationships lead to stronger feelings of happiness and healthier lives, while enriched environments stimulate neuroplasticity—the ability of the brain's neural networks to change through reorganization and growth. The ability of the brain to rewire and remap itself via neuroplasticity is profound.
- As adolescents mature, if they know how to keep developing the *positive* skills and activities that release dopamine, they are less likely to participate in high-risk behaviors. Dopamine, when released in a positive sense, will reinforce goal-directed activity. Indeed, our brains release extra dopamine when an experience is enjoyable.
- Positive humor boosts the vitality of our thoughts and emotions, and enhances our ability to deal with stress, anxiety, and depression.
- As the prefrontal cortex matures, adolescents are increasingly capable of moral reasoning and idealism. They are not irrational. Their reasoning abilities are likely to be developed *by the age of fifteen*, so, if they pause and think, they *can* logically assess whether or not an activity is dangerous. They are learning how to look not only at the reality of the world in which they live, but also how it could be.
- Physical activity builds brain cells, enhances the development of cognitive processing skills, and creates strong memory pathways.
- Where a young person grows up in a highly stressful and non-nurturing environment, their brain develops a greater sensitivity to stress, and less of a tendency for healthy, nurturing behavior.

Sometimes we just need to grit our teeth and speak to the potential we know is within a young person even when they seem unable to see it, or possibly even believe it. Persevere.

Do you have a story to share? Did you nearly quit on someone? What happened?

WEEK 18

Winning Ways to Achieve One's Potential

Choose happiness. Yes, it is a choice.

Here are some key thoughts for self-reflection, or to share with others trying to find their way. They can be used to encourage oneself or others to take responsibility, and become accountable for their choices.

Each of these points can create great discussion points with anyone you are privileged to mentor.

- I follow a healthy and balanced lifestyle.
- I am working to become a genuinely positive person with a positive self-image.
- I know myself, back myself, and believe in myself—I am capable and lovable.
- I am living for today and taking responsibility for my life.
- I believe in myself more and more each day.
- I am a dreamer imagining where I will be in one month, three months, or five years from now.
- I have set my specific, measurable, realistic, achievable goals, and have a timetable for achieving them.

- I am enjoying life to the full, making good friends, and reaching out to others in need of help.
- I am working at my self-discipline.
- I know my strengths and the areas I need to improve.
- I am unafraid to make decisions, and think things out for myself, while appreciating feedback in areas I could improve.
- I am flexible, and a good team player.
- My behavior is consistent and predictable *most* of the time.
- I am developing the qualities of trustworthiness, honesty, humility, empathy, and self-reliance.
- I enjoy my work, and am comfortable and self-confident in the company of others.
- I am prepared to take calculated and non-life-threatening risks.
- I dare to be different.
- I am prepared to move out of my comfort zone.

The legendary basketball coach John Wooden provided one of the best definitions of success, a great quote to share with anyone you are mentoring, or encouraging to achieve their potential. "Success is peace of mind which is a direct result of self-satisfaction in knowing you make the effort to become the best of which you are capable."

What matters is when we give a challenge our best shot, and have nothing left to give. We reach the end of the challenge, or the end of the day, and ask ourselves: "Have I done my best today?"

Enjoy the journey and the challenges ahead, and remind yourself that you never walk alone.

Do you have any points to add to these winning ways to share with your mentee?

WEEK 19

Practical Tips for Positive Parenting and Stress Management

Control your thoughts. They are more valuable than gold.

As we move further into the twenty-first century, researchers are telling us that the need for mentors will be a significant factor in the development of people.

As things stand now, there are insufficient mentors for all the young people in need of non-judgmental, empathetic wise guides to walk alongside them for a while.

These mentors will help them set some realistic, measurable, and achievable goals, and be that person who cares for them unconditionally, values their opinions, and helps them find a purpose for their lives.

Mentors, though, need to look after their own health and well-being and, through doing so, they model what life can be like for their mentees.

Mentors have true stories to share with their mentees, describing their life journey, the ups and downs, and how they have reached the place where they are mentoring other young people.

I stumbled across some useful tips for parents some years ago. As I have reflected more and more on them, I think they also embrace the spirit of mentoring. With a tweak here and a tweak there, perhaps they will be an encouragement to all who have the spirit of mentoring within their hearts.

PARENTING AND MENTORING TIPS

Someone said, "Never borrow from the future. If you worry about what may happen tomorrow and it doesn't happen, you have worried in vain. Even if it does happen, you have to worry twice."

- Pray with a special focus on giving thanks for all you have, who you are, and how you can most effectively reach out to others with unconditional love.
- Go to bed on time, and make sure you have the sleep your body needs (this differs from person to person).
- Get up on time so you can start the day unrushed.
- Say "No" to projects that won't fit into your time schedule, or that will compromise your mental health.
- Delegate tasks to capable others.
- Simplify and unclutter your life.
- Allow extra time to do things, and to get to places.
- Pace yourself. Spread out big changes and difficult projects over time; don't lump the hard things all together.
- Take one day at a time.
- Live within your budget.
- Have backups. As examples, an extra car key in your wallet, an extra house key buried in the garden, and extra tissues stored in the car.
- K.M.S. (Keep Mouth Shut). This single piece of advice can prevent an enormous amount of trouble, most especially when working with confused and vulnerable teenagers.
- Do something for the *kid in you* every day.
- Carry a spiritually enlightening book or eBook with you to read while waiting in line.
- Eat right—healthy food.
- Get organized so everything has its place—this also involves planning well, and prioritizing.
- Listen to music while driving that can help improve your quality of life.

- Write down, or electronically capture thoughts and inspirations, not only to keep fueling your energy, but also to share with your mentee.
- Every day, find time to be alone, with all technology switched off. Not only do you need to master reflective time, but you also can coach your mentee to develop this special time in a day.
- Having problems? Talk to God on the spot. Try to nip small problems in the bud. Don't wait until it's time to go to bed to try and pray.
- Make friends with non-judgmental people you trust.
- Keep a folder of favorite motivational sayings on hand—these can provide a great discussion starter with a mentee.
- Laugh.
- Laugh some more! Teach your mentees how to laugh at themselves too.
- Take your work seriously, but not yourself at all.
- Develop a forgiving attitude (most people are doing the best they can), and coach your mentee about the importance of forgiveness, and how to positively resolve conflicts.
- Be kind to unkind people (they probably need it the most).
- Sit on your ego, and practice humility.
- Talk less; listen more.
- Slow down—make a point each and every day to pause and reflect; smell the roses. This is a discipline your mentee can choose to learn as well.
- Remind yourself that you are not the general manager of the universe.
- Every night before switching off the light, think of one thing you're grateful for that you've never been grateful for before.

—Adapted—source unknown

While not everyone reading this will share my faith walk and references, there are enough words of encouragement and tips to grasp, and to reflect on when you are wobbling along yourself.

Do you have any additional tips to share with your mentee?

WEEK 20

'She Helped Me Gain Self-Confidence...' Life-Changing Moments

Embrace the creative spirit by seeing things in a new way.

I often ask the question: when you were a teenager, who, other than your parents and friends, had a significant influence on your life? Were there any life-changing moments?

Sometimes, sadly, some of the people I spoke to were living in homes that were not functioning too well for a variety of reasons, and positive parental influence was lacking.

No matter what the situation, most young people will talk about a teacher or a coach, a person who cared about them, believed in them, and was often a cheerleader during a confusing time of their life.

I recall the time a colleague died. We had taught together for five years, shared many life and teaching experiences, and enjoyed many laughs. Several of his former students left tributes thanking him for the different ways he touched their lives. Words and phrases like, "inspiring," "approachable," "friendly," "great teacher," "caring," and "great sense of humor," are littered throughout the tributes. Clearly one dedicated teacher impacted many more lives than he probably realized.

How often do we actually pause to hear from young people? "What do you think?" "How are you feeling?" "How can I help?"

Every day our global community mourns the death of many innocent lives, and the devastating injuries others have sustained as a result of bomb blasts, and shootings in different parts of the world. Nor should we forget the millions of young people living in poverty, or traumatized by war, or child abuse, or some other distressing event in their lives.

For many years I looked for different approaches to inspire and positively impact the lives of young people, encouraging them to use their God-given talents to fulfil their potential—the quiet ones who retreat into their shell, who perhaps lack confidence, who need to be reminded that they can take charge of their lives—and suggesting strategies they could attempt.

A number of quotes from students, aged fourteen and fifteen, who participated in the GR8 Mates school-based mentoring trial program—which I developed and facilitated—a while ago continue to inspire and motivate me.

Most of these students were displaying signs of disconnecting from school before they joined the program, many of them in single parent families and from low socio-economic, often high-risk environments.

All the volunteer mentors were appropriately trained, and received weekly encouragement and guidance during their active involvement in the mentoring journey.

The focus of the six-to-nine month mentoring relationship—a pity we did not have more time—was on connecting, sharing ideas about goals, and setting some personal best goals, looking at possible career options, and researching information on careers that interested the mentee.

Where possible, the mentor took the mentee to visit a company, or organization of interest to that young person from a career perspective.

This mentoring journey highlighted the importance of the choices we make in life. We choose our attitude when we wake up each day. We choose the people to move alongside us, and encourage us to chase our dreams.

As I read through the quotes below, I was again struck by the importance of relationships in these young people's lives, *face-to-face relationships*, not online interactions. With the development of the digital footprint, it is easy for us to forget that the most significant relationships are developed around three key words: *respect, empathy,* and *sincerity,* qualities that are shouting out to me when I read these quotes.

SHE HELPED ME GAIN SELF-CONFIDENCE

"[My mentor] has helped me through good times and bad and has helped me cope. She has also helped me with what my goal is in life and things I need to do to achieve becoming a teacher..."

"[My mentor] gave me a lot of confidence. He told me about my self-worth and my values. I was extremely lucky to get him as a mentor. I liked that I had someone to talk to whenever I needed to, through email and face-to-face. I realized throughout the journey my career goals and opportunities."

"My mentor has helped me analyze myself and the careers I'm interested in and helped me to find better time managing skills. I liked having someone to talk to about life in general, and having someone who can relate to certain things has been helpful and fun."

"She has really helped me with managing my time. She has also been a great help with finding information about my career and how to achieve it."

"She has helped me find what I'd like to do when I'm older and set a goal, as well as helping me find work experience at good places."

"I am now 100 percent sure about where I'm going in life and have gained many valuable skills that will help me achieve my goals... gained a friend."

"It was just good to be able to talk to someone about anything."

"He has helped sort through my life and make right decisions when it comes to work related things. Very awesome person. Really been good with him."

"[She] helped me gain self-confidence, realize what I wanted to do in the future, how I was going to get there and has helped me achieve my goals."

"She told me things I just wanted to hear."

"She has opened my mind to the opportunities and still has more I'd love to learn from her. She took me to a career psychologist showing me what I am best at. She has helped open my mind..."

"[She] has helped me become more confident in myself and I hope that I have made a positive impact on her life as well. I wish her all the best... talking about each other's lives, resolving issues and having a good laugh."

"She has helped me write my resume. She organized work experience. Good rapport."

"[She] has taught me to control my anger and shown me the importance of a good career."

I remember how one of these mentors went through personal difficulties a few years after this mentoring relationship began. On a social media platform the mentee, by then a young adult, posted a comment to the effect that, just as her mentor had been there for her during her confusing adolescent years, now she would be there to support her mentor.

The seeds of the spirit of mentoring had been successfully sown during these relationships.

Have you remembered who, other than your parents, made a significant and *positive* impact on your life when you were a teenager? Have you thanked them?

How are you inspiring a young person to chase a dream?

WEEK 21

'No Words Can Express My Gratitude Towards You . . .' Reaching Out

Learn to be comfortable in your own skin.

When you were a teenager, did you ever come across an adult who crushed your dreams? How did you react? What life lessons did you learn from that experience?

Fortunately, all the people who nurtured me as a young person encouraged me to chase my dreams; through the ups and downs, and the unpredictable winding paths of life's journey. I shall always be grateful to those cheerleaders.

"Cindy wanted to be a paramedic, but I crushed her dream and told her to do nursing," Cindy's mum shared with me. "And now Gemma wants to go into law, or something like that, and I am trying to get her to do nursing. I crushed Cindy's dream, and now I am crushing Gemma's dream. You know, I think she could be a great teacher!"

I found it challenging to have this conversation with Cindy and Gemma's mum. "Never crush a dream," I said. "Perhaps your thoughts explain why Gemma is a little confused about the career she should follow."

Anyone working with young people will have heard many stories like this. We should encourage young people to chase *their* dreams. The dreams will reveal a passion and, once that passion is identified, it is easier for teenagers to set realistic and achievable goals, and feel that their lives have purpose and meaning.

This underlines the importance of sowing the seeds of the spirit of mentoring when we are working with young people especially, although there are some common threads that cross all mentoring relationships.

EIGHT STRATEGIES TO DEVELOP MEANINGFUL RELATIONSHIPS

Here are eight strategies to develop meaningful relationships with teenagers. It is a useful check-list for a mentor reflecting on how the mentoring relationship is progressing.

1. Accept and appreciate your mentee as a young person, even though you may not accept their behavior. That involves offering unconditional love and care.
2. Display empathy toward your mentee—place yourself in their shoes and think about how they are feeling about whatever you are discussing. Remember your teenage years?
3. Respect your mentee for *who* they are, and also respect privacy. Mutual respect is likely to foster trust and confidence.
4. Be prepared to lead in keeping the lines of communication open, especially during times of conflict.
5. Display trust in your mentee. Work hard to establish this trust. It is an important process on the way to establishing a two-way mentoring relationship.
6. Be able and willing to fearlessly reveal your own personality to your mentee. Sometimes your openness helps your mentee see that you have been there, done that, and learned from the experience.
7. Be spontaneous and natural when relating with your mentee.
8. Have fun, don't take life or yourself too seriously, and take pleasure in each other's company.

Sometimes the relationship-building process can be hard work, though I always try and keep the fun element, possibly because I know that a sense of humor is one of my resilient qualities.

I received a thank you card from Nick about two months before he finished his schooling: "No words can express my gratitude towards you and all your help this year. I honestly don't think I could have done it without you. Here's to the final stretch."

What did I do?

I sat down with a young man trying to find his way, became a cheerleader, helped him set and achieve some personal and realistic goals, allowed him to dictate the pace of building this relationship, and we had a few laughs.

When Nick wanted to speak to me, I made myself available. On occasions, always with his permission, we had some tough chats about what it means to step up, and work hard towards fulfilling one's potential, and the choices we make along the way.

Also, with Nick's permission, I networked with his mum, thus ensuring that Nick was receiving consistent messages from some of the adults in his life. A partnership between parent, student, educator, or mentor is incredibly powerful in a teenager's life journey.

Nick had a dream of playing professional basketball in the USA. Many thought he was crazy.

My time spent with Nick was fascinating, frustrating, and an incredible journey for a young man with talent, "get up and go," a friendly personality, yet who struggled to fully appreciate what was needed to achieve one's dreams.

However, he was willing to learn, and eventually achieved his dream of playing professional basketball.

Building meaningful relationships lies at the heart of mentoring young people.

Who did you build a meaningful relationship with as a teenager? Did you have someone special who encouraged you to chase your dreams? If so, you have an important story to share with teenagers.

WEEK 22

One Day They Will Thank You

Make a difference to one. The many will follow.

How many times have you felt connected to someone, the relationship has wobbled somewhat, and you wanted to walk away?

How many times have you been in a formal or informal mentoring relationship with a younger person, and wanted to give up on them?

Have you actually walked away from a mentoring relationship, as you felt you had given your all? This would be a very normal and human thing to do.

I think back over the years to the many students I have either formally or informally mentored, the multiple times I have wanted to quit, and never did.

Researchers Karen Reivich and Andrew Shatte remind us of the importance of moving alongside young people: "Today's children, perhaps more than ever, need to learn how to solve problems, negotiate relationships, and persevere in the face of adversity. They need to be taught resilience."[1]

I recall deliberately putting some distance between myself and Graeme. This was more of an informal mentoring relationship. He then asked for a catch-up chat. I had thought he was not interested in communicating with me any longer.

---

1. Reivich and Shatte, *The Resilience Factor*, 253.

I made a similar decision with Sandy—also, more of an informal mentoring relationship—thinking that she was in a good headspace, and I could quietly slip further into the background. She, too, approached me and said it had been a while since we had chatted, and could we make a time to catch up?

If I thought hard enough, there would probably be more similar stories.

I did not give up on these students, simply eased back, and waited to see what would happen. If nothing had happened, I would have called each for a chat, simply to bring to an end a formal relationship, whilst letting them know I remained available should they ever wish to have a chat.

It's important that adolescents never feel someone is quitting on them, most especially in a formal mentoring relationship, as the mentor might be the *only* significant adult in their lives.

Those experiences reminded me that young people hear everything we say and, even if they are unable to verbally express it, they know when they have a non-judgmental cheerleader in their lives.

Another important point to remember is that as the prefrontal cortex—the decision-making area of the brain—is still developing during the adolescent years, one must never be afraid of repetition when having discussions.

Some neuroscience research is at pains to remind us how important it is to repeat things over a period of time, as this will build value into the development of the brain.

What follows are a few points under some individual headings to show how mentors of young people can sow the spirit of mentoring seeds in general discussions, being unafraid of repetition.

This is what establishing a self-empowering experience for the mentee, while building resilience, is all about. The young person already has the power to make decisions, and the mentor guides them along that journey.

ENHANCING THE RELATIONSHIP BETWEEN MENTEES AND THEIR PARENTS

- carry out household chores efficiently;
- be honest;
- share with your parents what's happening in your life;

- do all your school work without having to be reminded;
- take responsibility for the choices you make in life;
- be accountable for your actions;
- think before you act (make smart choices).

ENHANCING THE MENTEE'S EXPERIENCE OF SCHOOL LIFE AND ACADEMIC STUDIES

- get to know a teacher or counsellor, or at least one other adult who seems interested in your well-being;
- get connected to your school by joining a team, club, community, or cultural group—or some aspect of the extracurricular program;
- speak respectfully to authority figures;
- involve your parents in your school life as much as possible;
- choose positive friends who motivate you to achieve your potential, and support you to make good choices;
- model responsible behavior.

ENHANCING THE MENTOR'S RELATIONSHIP WITH THE MENTEE — TIPS FOR MENTORS

- be observant;
- be prepared to make a fool of yourself;
- never lose your sense of humor;
- fire those creative spirits;
- affirm one another;
- listen with empathy for the unexpressed feelings.

ENHANCING THE EMOTIONAL CONNECTION BETWEEN THE MENTOR AND THE MENTEE

- give your mentee your full attention;
- make eye contact (as culturally appropriate), and hold it for a few seconds at a time;
- be relaxed and not rushed—this is your mentee's time;
- express your feelings: smile, laugh out loud, feel the disappointment, anger, sadness—let it show in your tone of voice, facial expressions, and body language;
- identify strengths, and name them;
- tell your mentee when you are feeling pleased, encouraged, excited, disappointed, or sad for them, always doing your best to remain empathetic.

Clinical professor and well-known author Daniel J. Siegel writes: "When we have supportive relationships, we are not only happier, we are healthier and live longer . . . numerous studies support this idea that the more we help others, the healthier and happier we ourselves become."[2]

Persist through the challenging times, and have patience. One day that young person will thank you for standing by them during a tough season of their lives.

---

2. Siegel, *Brainstorm*.

WEEK 23

'This Is Your Calling and Your Gift.'

Use affirmation to keep motivated.

How do you reach out to someone who is struggling? How do you respond to someone who asks for your help? How do you speak messages of hope into the life of someone who feels hopeless? How do you offer a hand up, not a handout?

How do you ever know if your efforts have positively impacted a life?

Over many years I have journeyed alongside people of all ages, which has helped me fine-tune some important skills and qualities to build meaningful relationships:

1. Empathy—being able to put myself, to the best of my ability, in the shoes of the person with whom I am communicating.

2. Resiliency—identifying strengths and being able to bounce back; sharing with a person how to do this, and watching lives transformed before my eyes.

3. Communication—the importance of tone of voice, body language, eye contact, and being an excellent listener. Through face-to-face conversations with those I have mentored, I have coached them how to develop these qualities for themselves.

4. Humor—not taking myself too seriously, and remembering the importance of having fun and being able to laugh at myself, while also teaching people to learn how to laugh at themselves.

5. Goal-setting—sharpening the skills required to be an effective goal-setter and then a goal-getter chasing dreams. Again, I have seen lives transformed when wobbling people learn how to do this.

6. Persevering—learning over the years *never* to quit on anyone.

7. Non-judgmental—learning how to be non-judgmental, which is sometimes hard, yet developing this skill so people feel confident to open up, share their feelings, and trust me.

8. Cheerleading—one of my favorite roles, being the non-judgmental cheerleader speaking to the potential the confused person often cannot see.

9. Making a positive difference—believing that every person is essentially a good person who can positively influence others, and being prepared to walk alongside them as that encourager and cheerleader.

10. Empowering—coaching, teaching, and guiding people how to understand that every choice they make has a consequence. As they journey through life, they come to appreciate that, even though they already have the power to make choices, this is also a *self-empowering* journey.

11. Being vulnerable—knowing when and how to be vulnerable with anyone; watching people learn over time how to be vulnerable, and seeing some amazing transformations occur.

12. Faith—ego (edge God out)—I have seen many lives negatively impacted by the decision to go it alone; to become self-absorbed, the ultimate controller. My faith journey has taught me selfless servant leadership, and made me a stronger, more humble, caring, and compassionate person (who still has lots to learn).

13. Relationships—without meaningful relationships built on respect, empathy, and sincerity, most people will struggle.

14. Messages of *hope*—appreciating the importance of sharing messages of hope in the lives of all those with whom I interact.

How do you ever know if your efforts have positively impacted a life?

This was the question I posed earlier and, as a retired teacher, I am humbled when I hear from a student I taught many years ago, and who shares how something I did or said positively impacted their life.

While writing this musing, I received an email from Ron, now middle-aged and a successful business owner, who I taught over forty years ago, and who discovered that I had written books about mentoring.

Ron lacked self-confidence as a teenager, and I helped him along the way. He wrote:

> You truly *believed* in me! You showed me that nothing was impossible, that with hard work and commitment I could achieve anything that I wanted... You identified the fact that I was willing to work and wanted to succeed. You took me under your wing and with lots of extra lessons you helped me achieve an 'A' for History. Well, that 'A' has been a beacon of my success in later life... proving to me that I am very capable and that I can achieve with hard work, commitment and dedication.
>
> Your confidence and belief in me [through coaching sport] really built me up and has helped carry me and gave me courage and strength through good and tough times in my life. Back in the 1970s you mentored me as a young boy, and there was never a teacher who even came close to you in terms of your teaching ability, your mentoring ability, your dedication and passion for your work and everything you engaged in.
>
> It does not surprise me that you have dedicated much of your life to mentoring. This is your calling and your gift! Thank you, Robin, for the person that you are. Thank you for believing in me! I have always wanted to tell you this, and am so pleased that I am now able to do so.

I had no idea that my interactions with Ron had impacted his life in the ways he shared. It's moments like these that make teaching such a wonderful profession, and why promoting the spirit of mentoring is so important.

Who are you reaching out to today?

WEEK 24

10 Proven Strategies to Become an Effective Mentor

Take up another's burdens as your own.

Can you name one leader who has significantly impacted your life in a positive way? What happened?

While enjoying a cup of coffee, I was reflecting on the many leaders I have either worked under or met during the past five decades. Who were the leaders I had the most respect for? What specific management or leadership qualities, or skills did they possess?

A few of these people mentored me during different seasons of my life. Anthony Mallett, my school principal, taught and coached me how to stand up for my beliefs with courage and boldness, and that leadership came at a cost.

Professor John Morris, Chair of the Board of a school where I was the principal, modeled how to chair meetings, cut to the chase, yet respect the opinions of all. He was a compassionate and caring leader, though tough, and always fair.

Mike Denness, who later captained the England cricket team, coached me *never* to accept a half-hearted effort, and to keep striving to reach my potential.

10 PROVEN STRATEGIES OF AN EFFECTIVE LEADER

Here are ten strategies I collated from my research over the years, and from my personal experiences.

1. *Value all colleagues:* treat all colleagues equally and fairly; set time aside to affirm them personally and collectively; thank them sincerely when they have gone the extra mile; always use the words, "please", and "thank you", preferably alongside their names; a positive email or message of appreciation and encouragement is always appreciated; celebrate their birthdays and other special occasions.

2. *Be an excellent listener* who always respects their colleagues' opinions, ideas, feelings, and frustrations. Accept that a colleague might have good ideas that could work, or proven experiences to benefit the organization. Keep an open mind, and be flexible.

3. *Make sure all roles are clear, and that each member of the team knows what others are doing, and promote a spirit of collaboration.*

4. *Have fun!* Learn to laugh, especially at yourself. Greet each team member at the beginning of the day with a smile, and say "farewell" at the end of the day (where possible). Don't take life or yourself too seriously.

5. *Be sensitive and empathetic.* A positive experience is to walk in the shoes of a colleague for a while. Don't be afraid to apologize if a mistake has been made. Colleagues need to see that their leaders are authentic, yet fallible human beings.

6. *Be proactive, not reactive.* This requires one to be well organized, and in touch with team members, their circumstances, feelings—their stories. Remember, there *is* a solution to every problem or challenge. Never allow conflict situations to simmer, and turn every conflict situation into a positive learning experience whenever you can. Listen. Discuss. Consult. Be non-judgmental, and continually strive to be an authentic role model.

7. *Be well organized.* This involves prioritizing, planning, and staying on top of one's administrative load; knowing when colleagues are under pressure, and acknowledging this, even protecting them from others; following effective management of time practices. Respond to emails and messages from colleagues promptly, as this shows they are both respected and valued.

8. *Conduct competency reviews on time.* This improves performance and personal development. Look to turn the competency review into a positive growth experience for all concerned.
9. *Have an "open door" policy.* Always be approachable. If a colleague needs to offload to talk, make that person a priority in your life. Sometimes a colleague might simply want to share what's on their mind, and is not expecting any advice. At other times they might want some guidance, even reassurance.
10. *Encourage the personal development of colleagues.* Promote the idea of attending courses, conferences or workshops, and budget for these. Have the humility to accept that some colleagues have significant leadership skills, and are keen to develop these further to advance their career.

Do you have any stories to share about those who have been positive leaders in your life?

How will you share these strategies with your mentee, and help develop a positive person of influence?

WEEK 25

The Power of Goal-Setting

Surround yourself with great people.

How do you feel when you achieve a personal best goal?

I feel like celebrating somehow, especially when I have had to stretch myself, and move out of my comfort zone. Each small step I took helped me on the journey to achieve my goal.

Sometimes I stumble and fall, but hold on to my picture, imagining myself achieving the goal. I get up again, and move on. I never fail, just learn that something I have attempted did not work. What can I learn from that experience as I move on?

Ultimately, it is my *effort* that is more important than the outcome, as the effort shapes my personality and character. Leading coach for young women Julie Carrier comments:

> Real achievement means embracing the mess—recognizing that uncertainty, mistakes, confusion, setbacks, and lessons learned are not roadblocks, they are stepping-stones to reaching your goals, and more importantly, learning how to become your best version of you along the way.
> —Julie Carrier[1]

---

1. Advani and Goldsmith, *Modern Achievement*.

If we can remember how we became goal-getters, we have a story to share with our mentees, many of whom will need support to embark on a goal-getting program.

Most neuroscience research points to the importance of setting goals as a significant phase of brain development.

I was reminded recently of the variety of goals achieved by young people in mentoring relationships in programs with which I have been linked. These examples might encourage mentors, and help them to appreciate that there are a variety of goals one can encourage in a mentoring relationship, some of which are fairly straightforward, yet can create life-changing moments.

- A mentee's grades in one academic subject improved from 28 percent to 50 percent in a few months.
- A mentee worked on lifting weights at a gym, which the mentor used to teach goal-setting. They enjoyed a great relationship.
- A mentee and mentor—armed with the mentee's resume—visited shops in a shopping mall, picking up job applications as they went. The mentee gained a job that same day, thus achieving a goal without having written any goal-setting steps. The connection between mentor and mentee provided a foundation to build on for the remaining months of their mentoring journey together.
- A mentee worked at aerobic fitness as she was to be a bridesmaid later in the year. She lost weight and improved her self-image, which her mentor determined from her increasingly positive body language, and attitude to life.
- An overweight mentee, who wanted to exercise, went fishing with his mentor and the mentor's young family on the mentee's birthday. The mentor gave his mentee a gift voucher. On arriving home from the outing, the mentor received a phone call from his mentee saying that he had already bought fishing gear with the gift voucher. The mentee gained in self-esteem, improved his academic work, and improved his fitness which was kickstarted through his fishing experiences, and the mentor's encouragement.
- A mentee, after encouragement from the mentor, started attending the homework center at school, which led to academic improvement and, consequently, increased self-esteem.

- A mentor drew up a goal-setting strategy on the computer with his mentee, who was interested in computers.
- A mentee committed himself to read one novel a week to improve his English, with encouragement and support from his mentor.
- A mentee joined the local library with the help of the mentor.
- A mentee set up an exercise program with the help of the mentor.
- A mentee visited a computer firm, learned how to rebuild computers, and then set up his own small business from home.
- A mentee applied for a job, but was rejected. This was a major setback for the mentee, though the mentor encouraged her to persevere. Six months later, and with a better attitude, she applied for a new job with the help of the mentor, and was employed.
- A mentee (like many others) built her goals around obtaining a driver license.
- A mentee worked towards obtaining an overseas study scholarship. Her mentor helped her to prioritize, plan, and move out of her comfort zone to undergo new experiences.

Mentors who are new to mentoring would be encouraged to start with easily achievable goals, for example, getting to school on time for five successive days (if lateness for school is an issue). Achieving this goal develops the mentee's self-confidence, and can lay the foundation for more new experiences for the mentee during the mentoring journey.

Did you have anyone who guided you on a goal-getting journey at any time in your life?

How did they do this? How did you feel? Did you achieve all your personal best goals?

Do you still set goals?

WEEK 26

The Transformative Power of Mentorship: Celebrating Influential Teachers

Recruit a solid team for they will be needed in times of trouble.

Can you think of just one teacher who positively impacted your life?

That's a question I asked myself when my teaching career was coming to a close, and I entered retirement. I ended up reflecting on my education journey as a child through to becoming a young adult, and was amazed at my conclusions.

While I was a child recovering from cancer, most of my teachers were sympathetic and kind towards me, as I have shared in other weekly musings throughout this book. Of course, I appreciated their support, but that's not really what I was considering.

Which teachers shaped, molded, refined, disciplined, coached, mentored, and nurtured me? From the time I entered pre-primary school to completing my school days, there were at least fifteen teachers who positively impacted my life—quite an amazing thought.

This person might have been a sport coach for six months, a class teacher for a year, another coach for a year or two, a subject teacher for a couple of years, or the equivalent of a house tutor for about three or four years.

My key point, though, is that we all have opportunities to find a teacher who can mentor and encourage us, no matter what the situation might be.

> Teachers work in challenging, constantly changing environments where they often feel overwhelmed and unappreciated by those they serve. Teachers are valuable, and their individual and collective contributions to the lives of students, families, and colleagues are significant.[1]

The word *relationship* is fundamental to how we develop as young people.

In a November 2002 study *Finding Out What Matters for Youth*[2], which is still relevant today, Gambone, Klem and Connell identified two crucial elements that help young people reach healthy adult outcomes. Namely, young people benefit from:

1. *the availability of support and opportunities*—supportive relationships with adults and peers; challenging and engaging activities and learning experiences; and meaningful opportunities for involvement and membership;
2. *achieving developmental outcomes*—learning to be productive; to connect with adults, peers and social institutions; and to navigate through diverse settings, relationships and the lure of risky behavior. In all these areas, good outcomes for teenagers are strongly associated with success in early childhood.

In any setting, the authors suggested, what matters for the purpose of achieving developmental outcomes is that:

- relationships are emotionally supportive, with adults showing interest in young people's time and activities, and providing practical support with, for example, school work, or personal problems;
- activities are challenging, interesting, and related to everyday life;
- youth participate in decision-making in developmentally appropriate ways, relating to things they care about.

The spirit of mentoring involves encouraging mentees to link up with teachers and others with whom they interact, through academic studies,

---

1. Cox, *7 Key Qualities*, 1.
2. Gambone, Klem & Connell, *Finding Out*.

coaching a sport, music or dance, a club they might join, or some other extracurricular, or cultural activity.

And we, too, can share our personal experiences with our mentees to show them how we walked this adolescent road usually with the support of at least one significant adult.

STRATEGIES AND TIPS TO MAKE POSITIVE LIFE CHOICES

We can share lessons we have learnt from our interactions with others, and how we can take responsibility for the choices we make. Here are a few strategies and tips to share with mentees to help them make *positive* choices each day, and to live healthy lives.

- When I wake up in the morning, I can choose to spend a few moments thinking *positive* thoughts about the day ahead. Good health? Family? Grateful for food? An opportunity to be educated? A place to work? There is much to be thankful for.
- I can choose to connect with *positive* friends, family, and role models at every opportunity—to watch them, learn from them, be inspired and motivated by them.
- When I feel angry or in a bad mood, I can replace my negative thoughts with *positive* thoughts and pictures. If I choose to criticize, I can do so constructively, and without labelling people. When I choose to remain strong and calm, I am respected. If I choose to express anger, I will not use put-downs or violence.
- When I feel negative about a person, I can think about something *positive* to say. For a start, I can look at their good points.
- When I am feeling sorry for myself, moody, or depressed, I can think of something *positive* about myself and my surroundings. I can hold on to that *positive* thought for a while, and share my feelings with someone I trust. I can take a walk or run; go somewhere different; play some music that inspires me; connect with a friend through social media; or watch an inspirational, or amusing YouTube, or video clip. I can remember my dream photograph of who I am becoming.
- When a friend is negative and not feeling too good about things, I can try to put myself in their shoes to understand how they feel. I can look for a *positive* way forward. I can share something *positive* about

them—who they are, why I value their friendship, and mention some positive qualities others see in them. I must be genuine.

- At the end of the day, I can spend a few minutes thinking about all that has happened during the day. Have I done my best today? What can I learn from any setbacks or obstacles? How can I turn an obstacle into a new opportunity? What one thing have I learnt today that will help me in the future? Which *positive* thoughts can I embrace?

Some of my teacher-mentors guided me on the importance of a strong work ethic; some coached me on how to develop my sporting skills; some mentored me on how to lead and positively influence others, and a couple assisted my spiritual development—each a powerful experience in itself.

How about you? What would you share with your mentee?

WEEK 27

Controller, or a Positive Person of Influence?

Love more, not just people or things, but yourself.

While enjoying a cup of coffee the other day, I was thinking about some of our world leaders, and wondered how many of them are authentic positive people of influence who show sincere care and compassion for *all* people? How many of them are, in reality, controllers?

Then I was thinking about how effective mentoring qualities could transform so many of our world leaders.

During my career as a teacher and an employee of some non-governmental organizations, I worked under a variety of leaders. Some were inspiring, wonderful team players, with servant leader hearts. Others were more egocentric, and continually wanted to be in the limelight.

Others lacked charisma, got the job done, enjoyed the privileges that came with the job, yet seldom inspired or motivated those under their guidance.

I have had the privilege of holding leadership positions for most of my life and suspect that, if you asked members of different teams which I led over the years to describe my leadership style, answers would probably result in a combination of the above descriptions.

That's the sad reality, though my hope is that most of them—especially in my later years with more maturity and life experiences—would say that I was first and foremost a team player who encouraged others to reach their potential.

I also hope that the majority would describe me more as a positive person of influence than as a controller. What's the difference?

A controller breeds fear, not trust, and feels threatened if someone stands up to them. Perhaps, deep, deep down there are some insecurities. They don't want people to know about these, so they build protective walls around themselves.

Those under the controller are reluctant to take calculated risks, as they fear the outcome.

As the controller is always right, they make assumptions which creates a lack of unity in a management team, and lots of superficial talk. There is little enjoyment or fun working in such an environment.

The controller does not wish to become too close to their employees or colleagues because they don't want to risk appearing vulnerable at any time. Therefore, they only encourage and develop people as far as the controller personality allows.

Think of all the unique gifts and talents of individuals that are squashed by a controller, and the world is the real loser.

Humans are designed to partner with others—to experience positive and significant relationships—and our brains need social connection to remain vital and healthy.

These are important points to remember, especially in the twenty-first century as the entrepreneurial spirit finds its feet, and the emphasis moves from individual to creative and innovative teamwork.

Conversations are not just a way of sharing and exchanging information, ideas, thoughts, or opinions. They actually trigger physical and emotional changes in the brain that either open us up to having a healthy, trusting conversation, or close us down so that we speak from fear, uncertainty, caution, and worry.

Co-creating conversations have the power to literally rewire our brains, hence the positive impact a leader can have on someone's life.

The key word, though, is *trust*, which neuroscientists tell us, is difficult to sustain when we are afraid to share our inner world. So, we need to know ourselves to be able to identify the signs of developing distrust before the amygdala is triggered.

An overactive amygdala will result in feelings of fear and distrust closing down our brain (perhaps that emotional explosion), as this is the part of the brain that protects us from harm, and is always listening for words and meanings that might threaten us.

Then we can activate higher brain functions in the executive brain, which results in feelings of empathy, judgment, and the development of more strategic skills (refer to the Week 17 musing for more brain information).

The result? We improve the *social connection* and can progress positively.

When we develop those strong bonds of trust, the brain releases the feel-good chemicals oxytocin, dopamine, and serotonin, with the probable result that we feel better, and more positive.

We feel more empowered to work out issues and challenges, and we are open to new experiences and ideas. Most important, self-empowerment results in better ownership of change.

Some research has suggested that the two least developed skills in the workplace are the ability to have uncomfortable conversations, and the ability to ask, "What if. . .?" questions.

These two skills are critical for building and sustaining trust and being open, honest, and caring with one another.

Remember, too, the importance of the non-verbal part of our conversations, critically important in the development of meaningful mentoring relationships. In many ways it is more important than the actual verbal element in defining the meaning of our interactions—body language, eye contact, and tone of voice, all of which assist in creating that atmosphere of trust.

Some tips from my research to encourage personal and leadership development—become a positive person of influence—focus on the development of skills like the following:

1. *Build rapport* by focusing on getting on the same wavelength as the person with whom you are communicating.
2. *Listen without judgment*—this involves paying full attention to the other person as they speak, while consciously setting aside the human tendency to judge that person.

3. *Ask discovery questions* which open the minds of others to the power of curiosity—and innovation—as well as to the possibility of changing our views as we listen and learn.

4. *Reinforce success*—in other words, focus on seeing (visualizing) and validating what *success looks like,* as this enhances connectivity and honest sharing.

5. *Dramatize the message*—when you struggle to connect through speaking, try another method such as story-telling, or showing a picture to help explain what you are thinking, and trying to share.

The spirit of mentoring lies at the heart of effective leadership, and mentors who strive to be people of positive influence can significantly impact the lives of the young people they mentor.

What are your leadership experiences?

WEEK 28

How to Build a Resilient Youth

Do something daring every day. You will open yourself to life's great adventure.

Resilience is a process of connectedness as competent and emotionally stable mentors link to their mentees, their interests, and their dreams and goals.

I am continually reminded of how important it is for young people to understand they are responsible for the choices they make each day.

Every choice has either a positive, or a negative consequence.

When young people are experiencing challenging times, or abuse of any sort, they can choose to speak to someone they trust, despite possible fears of the consequences of such decisions.

Their health and well-being are critical to reaching their *full potential*.

This is where a mentor—or a trusted adult—can be that non-judgmental wise guide on the side encouraging the growth and development of a young person.

When you connect with your mentees, as you do when you foster resiliency, you meet their emotional safety needs. While you cannot remove stress and adversity from their lives, providing them with emotional safety puts them in a position to develop problem-solving, and social skills.

As the mentees develop these skills, along with competence in an area of their choice, they strengthen their self-confidence, self-esteem, and sense of efficacy—the belief that they can master their environment, and effectively solve life's challenges.

With the help of a mentor, they can identify and develop personal strengths, and increase the skills to rally the resources they need to stay strong when adversity threatens to overwhelm.

The power of effective mentoring builds resilient young people. Mentees who connect with their mentor:

- are in a mutually caring, respectful mentoring relationship, in which the mentor encourages, and nurtures their resilient qualities;
- have opportunities for meaningful involvement;
- get along better with their parents or caregivers, and teachers (authority figures);
- develop a more positive attitude to life;
- achieve more at school, or in their place of work or study;
- develop a style of thinking—or a way of looking at the world—to determine their level of resilience, and the ability to overcome, steer through challenges, and to bounce back from adversity[1];
- reduce their drug usage, alcohol abuse, truancy, and other antisocial activities.

10 TIPS AND STRATEGIES TO BUILD A RESILIENT YOUNG PERSON

Family therapist, author and internationally recognized expert on resilience among youth and families, Michael Ungar[2], has shared many thoughts and ideas for building a resilient young person, which provide the framework for the following suggested tips and strategies for a positive mentoring relationship.

1. *Relationships:* Encourage your mentee to make a strong connection with at least one caring adult role model, other than their parent. Youth mentoring research encourages a young person to seek at least three significant adults who offer unconditional, non-judgmental care,

---

1. Reivich and Shatte, *The Resilience Factor*, 19.
2. Ungar, *Resilience Research*.

to become their cheerleaders or mentors during their adolescence. Teachers, coaches, grandparents, or close relatives can undertake this mentoring role. When this occurs, the young person develops important relationship-building skills.

2. *Control*: There are many important decisions mentees can make at every stage of their development. Be sure to give them the chance to feel what it's like to make decisions they're ready to make, and experience the consequences. Mentors should, therefore, refrain from offering advice for as long as possible. Encourage the young person to come up with solutions. They often surprise us.

3. *Expectations*: Mentees need to know that they are expected to do their best, whatever that best is. A mentee who doesn't believe anyone cares how well they do is a young person who might feel lost and alone. Mentors can identify and name specific strengths they discern in a young person. Talk about these and ensure that the young person takes ownership of them. Never accept a second-best effort.

4. *Identity*: Offer mentees genuine opportunities to show others what makes them unique. Sensitively guide them to accept that there are situations they can't change. Avoid superficial pats on the back that even the young person knows mean nothing. Share your stories to show *your* unique character, and then encourage your mentee to walk a similar journey with a spirit of hope and optimism.

5. *Safety and support*: No matter how chaotic life gets, remember that mentees cope best when they feel safe, secure, and certain about their next meal. Families should eat together at least three times a week. Mentors can talk about this with their mentees to gain a deeper understanding of the family dynamics.

6. *Contribution*: Offer mentees a chance to make a contribution to their communities. Volunteer activities ensure young people see themselves as capable and competent, while they gather around themselves a social network of peers and adults who see them as special. Mentors can model what volunteering looks like. Often powerful discussions between a mentor and a young person occur during such times of selfless service.

7. *Belonging*: The best way to make a mentee feel they belong is to give them a chance to show they have a place in [the] family. Does

the family have a pet? Who feeds and looks after it? This is a good conversation topic between a mentor and a mentee. Can the mentee cook dinner once a week, help look after a younger sibling, or babysit, or take on another responsible duty in the home?

8. *Culture*: Encourage mentees to share knowledge of their family and ancestors. A sense of pride in where they come from will follow. The best way to help a young person feel this pride is for them to share information about themselves in a safe, secure, and non-threatening environment. Let them bring a favorite family food to the next mentor gathering; do something traditional for a birthday celebration, or encourage them to invite friends to a cultural event. Some young people do not even know what careers their grandparents followed. Have them find out. This is another topic for informal discussion.

9. *Acceptance*: There are few things mentees crave more than acceptance. It's the foundation for attachment. Let your mentee know that they are welcome in your family, at their school, and in their community. Problem behaviors are often a cry for help. Accept that the young person is trying, as best as they can, to obtain what they need. You don't have to accept the specific problem behavior to still accept your mentee as someone worthy of your care and support. Mentors can play a significant role as the non-judgmental cheerleader, especially when the family dynamics might be difficult. Guide them how to stop being a victim and to create a positive future.

10. *Social Justice*: Teach mentees how to stand up for their rights. If there is a battle your mentees can fight for themselves, coach them how to argue respectfully for their rights. During this time also coach them how to "listen" respectfully, and with empathy. Mentors can play a key role in guiding young people how to positively resolve conflicts, handle social media, be responsible with regard to use of social media, and learn to tolerate and respect others who think differently.

Researchers Karen Reivich and Andrew Shatte remind us that: "Resilience transforms. It transforms hardship into challenge, failure into success, helplessness into power."[3]

---

3. Reivich and Shatte, *The Resilience Factor*, 4.

Remember, the mentor, too, must understand how the world works and thinks before they try and change it, or before they create the tune and melody to which they wish to dance each day.

WEEK 29

Build Meaningful Relationships

Appreciate everything you already have in life.

If you did not grow up with social media, can you recall any difference between how you communicated with others then, and how you communicate with others these days? How do you *most effectively* communicate with your mentees?

"Sally, you seem to spend a lot of time on your phone."

"Yes, I do."

"Are you addicted?"

"Yes, sometimes I think I am."

"Well, I watched you at sport last weekend. You went along to watch the sport, yet spent most of your time looking at your phone."

"I saw the sport."

"Yes, right!"

I had a conversation that went something like that with a student in her final year of school. We continued along these lines:

"Do you keep your phone in your bedroom overnight?"

"Yes."

"Do you keep your phone on through the night?"

"No, I turn it off at about 9.30 pm."

"And I am sure you have been on it on and off since 7.00 am?" I smiled.

"Yes, you're probably right."

Being addicted to social media appears to be an increasing issue emerging in the global world of adolescents, and that's probably a topic for another day.

This conversation helped me to reflect on how much better we communicated when I was an adolescent. We didn't have all the social media gadgets that don't show body language, tone of voice, and facial expressions, all key aspects of effective interaction between two people.

Constructive communication between a mentee and a mentor can radically improve their relationship. Face-to-face feedback can be potentially life-changing for some mentees, as influential pastor and mentor Howard Hendricks stated: "Experience is not the best teacher; *evaluated* experience is."[1]

So, when communicating constructively, don't forget the importance of giving feedback as a way of offering *constructive assistance*. It will enable you to:

- prompt your mentees to consider changing their behavior—for example, by giving feedback on how their behavior is affecting others;
- keep your mentees on track—for example, by giving feedback in relation to their personal best goals. Share with them Albert Einstein's belief from his personal experiences: "A person who never made a mistake never tried anything."

Your mentees also need helpful feedback in order to improve. If they do not understand their strengths and developmental needs, it is hard for them to know how to develop and learn.

In order to give feedback that is constructive:

- Give feedback at an appropriate time. Do *not* give feedback until you have established the correct climate, which is a strong, respectful, trusting relationship, and your mentee is in a positive headspace to receive feedback;
- provide a balance of positive and negative—and, if you need to criticize, attack the *behavior* rather than the *person*;
- be specific and descriptive;
- give relevant feedback;
- offer feedback that encourages further discussion.

1. Mwaura, *The Influential Mentor*.

I ask students if they want feedback, as they require a positive mindset to receive information, good or not-so-good and, by taking this approach, a form of self-empowerment occurs.

I hope that Sally reflected on her potential phone addiction, and spent more time talking face-to-face with her peers, and other adults.

What do you observe when watching adolescents in any situation these days? How do you positively respond to these situations?

WEEK 30

Life Lessons from Meeting a Nobel Peace Prize Winner

Forgive frequently. Forgiveness is not an occasional act. It is an attitude.

> There comes a point where we need to stop just pulling people out of the river. We need to go upstream and find out why they are falling in.
> —Desmond Tutu

There were a number of life lessons I learnt from the time I spent with Archbishop Desmond Tutu soon after he had been awarded the Nobel Peace Prize in 1984, which helped me on numerous occasions when coaching and mentoring young people.

At the time, I was teaching history at a boys' boarding school in the scenic midlands of Kwazulu-Natal in southern Africa. All staff were expected to facilitate a club or society, and I ran the African Affairs Society. A small group of senior students interested in discussing African affairs, with a focus on what was happening in apartheid South Africa, came together two or three times a quarter. We enjoyed many robust discussions.

The school had invited Anglican Archbishop Desmond Tutu to be a guest speaker, and I was asked if I would collect him from the airport, approximately a ninety-minute drive.

52 MENTOR MUSINGS

Tutu was the first black Anglican priest to be appointed Archbishop of Cape Town. He was an anti-apartheid and human rights activist who promoted non-violent protest, and an economic boycott of South Africa during the 1980s to bring about universal suffrage.

In 1984 Tutu was awarded the Nobel Peace Prize in recognition of his efforts to bring about peace in southern Africa. He accepted the award on behalf of the oppressed people in South Africa.

Author John Allen quotes a comment made by Tutu in 1985 at the height of the anti-apartheid struggle to explain his thinking:

> I have no hope of real change from this government [South Africa] unless they are forced. We face a catastrophe in this land and only the action of the international community by applying pressure can save us. Our children are dying. Our land is bleeding and burning and so I call the international community to apply punitive sanctions against this government to help us establish a new South Africa—non-racial, democratic, participatory and just. This is a non-violent strategy to help us to do so. There is a great deal of goodwill still in our country between the races. Let us not be so wanton in destroying it. We can live together as one people, one family, black and white together.[1]

Tutu played a key role in the fall of apartheid, and transitioning South Africa to a democratic country under the leadership of President Nelson Mandela. On his release from prison in 1990, Mandela described Tutu—at whose home he stayed on his first night of freedom—as the "people's archbishop."

Mandela later appointed Tutu as the chair of the Truth and Reconciliation Commission in South Africa, which played a significant role in seeing the country peacefully transition into a democratic nation.

When I collected Tutu at the airport, I was greeted by an unpretentious short man, friendly, open, and warm-hearted.

As we drove to the school, I commented on the fact that I had expected an international figure and Nobel Peace Prize winner to emerge through the gates of the airport accompanied by a couple of bodyguards, especially during the challenging political times in which we were living in South Africa.

Here was my first lesson as he chuckled and responded, "God has a wonderful sense of humor."

---

1. Allen, *Rabble-Rouser for Peace*.

He proceeded to tell me how much he enjoyed traveling to the US. He was treated like royalty, and transported in a large car with a police escort. He regarded the experience as great fun.

My second lesson was the importance of humility. Tutu was one of the humblest people I have ever had the privilege of meeting. He did not take himself too seriously, yet was authentic and passionate about the causes he supported.

The eyes and ears of many predominantly privileged—and fairly ignorant of the political realities in the country at the time—white boys were opened when Desmond Tutu shared his story with the school community that night. I recall reading many years later that one of those young lads acknowledged that one of the life-changing moments in his life was hearing and later chatting to Tutu that night.

Tutu's visit and the time I spent with him in the car, sharing thoughts and ideas, and tapping into his wisdom and life experiences, inspired me to launch South African Youth Symposia (SAYS).

During the next ten years, with the help of like-minded colleagues and students at the schools where I taught, I organized annual symposia attended by young girls and boys of all races and cultures from throughout South Africa.

The main purpose of these symposia was for these young people to come together to share stories, break down racial barriers, have fun together over three days, and to prepare for a post-apartheid South Africa, which was inevitable.

We invited controversial guest speakers to share their thoughts and ideas linked to a symposium theme. Students would then gather in non-racial groups, which had been organized prior to the symposium, to discuss questions set by the speaker, offer their feedback, and then enjoy an open discussion. There was plenty of time for fun activities, and informal chats.

Approximately six thousand students attended these symposia, which later included conflict resolution, and life skills workshops.

In addition, Hugh Huggett—to whom I have dedicated this book—a colleague from another school in Johannesburg, and I organized two non-racial field hockey tours to the U.K in the mid and late 1980s, during a time when there was a sports boycott of South Africa.

Our aim was to show members of the overseas community that there were schools in South Africa open to all races and cultures trying to make a positive difference.

We traveled under the name Kestrels.

Hugh Huggett was a teaching colleague, confidant, mentor and good friend and, like Tutu, who he also admired and respected, he was humble, and with a great sense of humor. Hugh was bold and courageous as he spoke out against apartheid and injustices, and spent many hours reaching out to disadvantaged young people, and speaking words of hope into their lives. Hugh actively exemplified the spirit of mentoring.

My time with Tutu always evokes cherished memories and brings a smile to my face. It was definitely one of the highlights of my life, another being when I attended a Prayer Breakfast in the London Houses of Parliament at which British Prime Minister Margaret Thatcher was present.

At this prayer gathering I met the Chief Minister of the Bantustan[2] KaNgwane, Enos Mabuza. A year or so later we worked together to find the site for a new non-racial school in KaNgwane, Penryn College. That's a story for another day.

In 1987 Tutu spoke on the tenth anniversary of the death of Phakamile Mabija in detention, commenting that suffering was unavoidable, especially for a Christian witnessing for Christ in a situation of injustice, oppression, and exploitation. He might have been describing his own life journey when he said:

> When we make the so-called preferential option for the poor; when we become the voice of the voiceless ones; when we stand in solidarity with the hungry and the homeless, the uprooted ones, the down-trodden, those that are marginalized, we must not be surprised that the world will hate us, and yet, another part of the world will love us.[3]

Archbishop Desmond Tutu, always a legend in my eyes; infectious humor, humble, compassionate, bold and courageous, with an unwavering faith, above all, a man of peace who died peacefully at the age of 90 in 2021.

Stories of courageous men and women fascinate most teenagers, and can lead to inspirational and motivational discussions about chasing dreams.

---

2. A Bantustan was a territory that the South African government set aside for black inhabitants of South Africa as part of its policy of apartheid.

3. Du Boulay, *Tutu, Voice of the Voiceless*.

WEEK 31

Mentoring Strategies Developed from My Life Journey[1]

Be grateful, not just for this day, but for every day.

Do you ever feel lost for words when a friend or colleague is facing a serious challenge in their lives?

Do you know anyone who has been struck down with cancer, or another incurable disease, or illness? Anyone who might be on that journey at the moment?

Do you know a young person needing encouragement? Someone, especially a teenager, struggling to adapt to the results of suffering from cancer, or some other serious illness, or the loss of a loved one?

There *is* a solution to every life challenge we face.

I was struck down with cancer at the age of nine and underwent radiation treatment (2.5 times the adult dose), followed by significant major surgery during the next couple of years, and then again when I was eighteen (see the Week 2 musing for more information).

After my first major surgery, my parents were told that I probably had two years to live and during these two years my mother died suddenly.

---

1. This musing has been adapted from Cox, CHOICES, 2–8

10 HELPFUL MENTORING STRATEGIES

Thankfully, I survived the cancer and now, in my retirement, and reflecting on my life journey to date, here are ten helpful mentoring strategies which I have learnt, through trial and error, highs and lows, over the years.

These strategies helped me through my challenging adolescent years as I came to terms with my disfigurement, and responded to it. Some of these I have already shared in the Week 2 musings. Repetition is deliberate.

1. *Attitude*—never forget that you choose your attitude and how you respond to the challenges that life throws at you. The choices you make will ultimately determine your future. Live with hope, and work hard at carrying a positive, constructive attitude into everything you do, and into all your significant relationships.

2. *Passion/s*—identify your passion or passions. If you could do anything you wanted today, and had all the qualifications you needed, what would you choose to do? That's likely to be your passion—do something with it. Create dreams and chase them. Windows of opportunity will open for you as you move out of your comfort zone.

3. *Self-discipline*—construct a disciplined, healthy, and balanced lifestyle. Some examples could include: having between seven and nine hours' sleep a night (depending on your age); managing your time well (time to work, time to study, time to reflect, time to eat, time to socialize and relax, time to exercise, time to follow an interest or hobby, time to sleep); following a healthy diet—breakfast is an important meal to provide the brain with the energy it requires to get through the day; saying "no" to drugs and alcohol abuse (so you don't damage your brain during crucial developmental times), cigarettes, vaping, and inappropriate behavior.

4. *Goal-getting*—be a goal-getter. Experiment with different methods of reaching your personal best goal, or goals until you find what works best for you. Share your ideals, passion, or passions and goals with someone you trust. Draw up a clear action plan and take small steps initially. Take ownership of your goals and envision yourself achieving them today—"I feel excited as I . . ." Research suggests that those who set goals achieve much. Include a goal that sees you reaching out to others and expecting nothing in return, and you can discover more positive qualities about yourself. Sometimes a simple gesture such as

a friendly smile directed at a stranger, or a peer, can change their day. Be proud of all you achieve, and always remain humble.

5. *Relationships*—keep building your relationships and networks with friends, family, other adults, or peers, or employers. When you surround yourself with positive friends you have a greater chance of reaching your full potential. Positive friends know right from wrong—always choose your friends carefully, and let trust develop over time. Find a mentor who will be a non-judgmental and caring wise guide; your consistent cheerleader. Be a team player—a sure way to develop positive relationships; have role models in your life; be an encouragement to others; turn obstacles into opportunities, and reach out to those in need.

6. *Communicate*—work consistently hard at developing and improving your communication skills. Become a brilliant listener, a motivator, encourager, and inspiration to others. Develop a positive vocabulary; watch your body language, and radiate unconditional care and compassion towards others. Show empathy, be genuine, and respectful, and people will value your contributions to their lives. Also learn how and when to be vulnerable in a safe and secure environment, allowing others to gain a deeper understanding of your feelings. Strive at all times to be trustworthy, a person of integrity, someone who keeps their word, and on whom others can depend.

7. *Conflict*—conflict is part of daily life. Learn how to turn conflict into a positive learning and growth experience. Deal with it without violating another's rights, and don't run away from conflict situations. Develop mediation skills. Become a healer, an agent of change, and a peacemaker where there is tension, pain, misunderstanding, and suffering. Be quick to sincerely forgive those who wrong you, even if you struggle to forget.

8. *Failure*—don't fear failure. Failure will teach you more about yourself, and your God-given talents and abilities. Move out of your comfort zone if the challenge is not life-threatening. Have the courage to learn from the experience. Life coach Julie Carrier states, "Courage means you feel the fear and move forward anyway. Courage is what develops confidence."[2] Engrave into your being that every obstacle can be turned into an opportunity if you are prepared to think creatively, seek the guidance and wisdom of those you trust, and have the patience to

---

2. Advani and Goldsmith, *Modern Achievement*.

work towards something, rather than expect a quick-fix solution, or display an attitude of instant gratification.

9. *Persevere*—don't quit! Go the extra mile even if you have to sweat a little. Make some sacrifices (of social life, perhaps), or commit yourself to something for a little longer. You will be amazed at what can be achieved when you do this. Take time out each day to think about how you are doing, what you are doing, why you are doing it, and what lessons can be learnt. Ten minutes of daily personal reflection could make a significant difference to the way you cope with life's challenges.

10. *Celebrate*—celebrate the small and big victories; the times you achieve a relatively simple goal, or achieve a long-term major goal, or when you successfully conquer a tough challenge. Laugh often (at yourself especially). Have fun. Remember the importance of gratitude during these special times—always express your genuine thanks to those who share their gold nuggets of wisdom and experience with you, or offer you a helping hand.

I have shared my experiences with teenagers I mentored, and encouraged them to keep on keeping on through the confusing adolescent years, especially when the odds are stacked against them.

I have also shared these experiences with adults who are facing challenges and needed some words of encouragement.

As you journey through life, work hard at your "mirror talk"—love the person you see in the mirror each day. Remind yourself every day, *"I am lovable and capable,"* and you will continue to develop your strengths and resilient qualities.

Remember, you are unique and special. Never forget that no-one has *your* specific gifts and talents. Ignore those who suggest otherwise.

Your story can inspire others and, despite your imperfections, you can become a light in their darkness, sharing messages of hope, setting on fire the hearts of struggling souls to overcome their personal challenges, and reach their potential.

We have the power to change the global narrative, and create a more compassionate and caring global community in which every life matters.

Do you have a story to share? Do you have a word to inspire others who are struggling?

Who can you encourage today?

To whom can you say: "You matter to me?"

WEEK 32

'When It Comes Down to It, We All Just Want to Be Loved.'

Happiness comes from within. Honor your feelings.

How do you react to fourteen-year-old John Yellin's comment in the title above?

What is it that tugs at your heart-strings, and leads you to interact with others? How do you express *selfless* love and care to those with whom you relate?

These are questions I have often asked myself as I collated my research on the adolescent brain, and interacted with a couple of adolescents who had asked me to mentor them.

There is much untapped talent among the youth in our global community.

There are days when I wish I had a magic wand and could connect with every young person who only wants to feel loved and cared for, reach out to them, and encourage them to become the best they can be.

This passion, which is deeply rooted in my heart and soul, led me to become a teacher, sports coach, set up youth mentoring programs, peer mentoring programs, train student leaders, and run life skills workshops for adolescents.

I recall a week, early in my retirement, during which I experienced four different moments that pulled at my heart-strings, and reminded me of the massive global need for mentoring programs, and support of our young people.

This is what I recorded at the time:

"I follow a fairly self-disciplined daily routine these days. I wake up and enjoy a cup of tea during a time of prayer and reflection, before I head off on a six kilometers old man's jog along the sea front, a good opportunity to reflect, and enjoy the beauty of the sunrise.

After a shower, I purchase the daily newspaper from the local news agent. I am a newspaper addict, not wanting the electronic version, rather the hard copy tabloid, which is better for my aging eyes.

Last week, while returning from the news agent, I passed a couple of bus shelters where young students were waiting for the bus to transport them to school. Some were listening to music, others were glued to their mobile phones, others stood quietly leaning against the bus shelter.

I wanted to stop the car and ask each student what their story was. "How are you feeling today? What are your hopes and dreams? How can I help you?" Of course, I did not do this, though I could tell from the body language of one or two students, they probably could do with some encouragement.

Then again, it was relatively early in the morning for most of them, and I wondered how many had had the all-important nine hours sleep?

The Voice is a popular Australian TV show, an opportunity for young and old to showcase their singing talents in the hope that they can progress through the show, gain coaching from experienced celebrities, and eventually become *The Australian Voice*.

What tugs at my heart-strings, though, are the stories shared by some contestants—how they had to overcome obstacles, tough times, families not functioning too well, bullying, or some other humiliating experience— such resilience. All these contestants would probably have benefitted from the presence of *a wise guide on the side* in their lives.

Another story making headlines at the moment is about a family tragedy in Queensland, Australia.

During the 2011 floods a mum and her teenage son were trapped in their car as the floodwater rose. While a younger son was rescued, the mum and teenage son were washed away, and drowned.

Questions are being asked about the investigation into the incident, and the failure of emergency personnel to be notified of what was going on when the mum called for help.

The surviving young son, now an adolescent, has dropped out of school and, according to his still grieving and angry dad, seems to have no purpose in life.

All I want to do is offer to mentor this young man, and take him to a place where he sees hope in the future, identifies some dreams, and begins to chase them.

My fourth moment was reading a post from the United States *Be a Mentor*[1] youth mentoring program on a social media platform, which began by pointing out that:

> 15 million children woke up today without a caring adult in their lives. Their environments are that of violence, gangs, drugs and educational deficiencies. Children of incarcerated parents typically go to jail. Dependents of welfare recipients typically become dependent on government subsistence. Youth who are substance abusers often die before contributing to society. And teenage parents have fewer options for success.

In New Zealand, where I live, this suggests that more than twice the population of this country, or over half the population of Australia have *no* caring person in their lives. This is a staggering statistic. I feel so helpless at not being able to do anything to be a global mentor to all these young people."

Those were some of my thoughts and experiences—always the idealistic dreamer—as mentioned earlier, during a week soon after I retired.

There are many ways to encourage our young people, and enhance our relationships with them, a response perhaps to John Yellin's comment. These might include:

- care for them unconditionally;
- laugh a lot, and have heaps of fun;
- celebrate birthdays;
- create a safe and secure environment, where they feel a sense of belonging;
- always turn up for meetings on time;

1. Be a Mentor, Inc.

- speak to the potential they might be unable to see at that particular time for a variety of reasons;
- do your best not to quit;
- hear *every* word with respect;
- value and acknowledge their suggestions, opinions, and ideas;
- celebrate their successes, no matter how small one success might appear to be (it could be massive in the young person's life);
- believe in them, and let them know this;
- identify and promote their resilient qualities and strengths;
- be open-minded and flexible;
- explore new options and opportunities together;
- teach and coach them that it's okay to make mistakes, while encouraging them to learn from the experience; always comment on their *effort* before considering an outcome;
- teach and coach them how to work through difficulties;
- inspire and share a sense of curiosity and creativity;
- always be available;
- stand alongside them no matter what.

Some years ago, Dr Emmy Werner, Research Professor of Human Development at the University of California, a global expert in the area of resiliency, shared some of the work she and others had undertaken following about seven hundred children on Kauai (Hawaii) over a thirty-year period.

Many of the children were growing up in high-risk areas of poverty where there was drug and alcohol abuse, and many other complex issues. Yet the overwhelming majority of them ended up gaining a sound education, and entering careers that allowed them to lead positive and stable lives.

What was significant in the development of these resilient young people, in addition to their competence in basic reading skills—which Werner stated was a critical factor in their personal development—was that most of them had found an adult mentor in their communities who became their non-judgmental cheerleader, and guided them through their adolescent years.

Werner concluded her time of sharing by saying:

> We've learned from them (the young people) that competence and confidence and caring can flourish, even under adverse circumstances. If children encounter persons who provide them with a secure basis for the development of trust, autonomy, initiative, and competence they can successfully overcome the odds. That success brings hope, *realistic hope*. And that is a gift each of us can share . . . The rediscovery of the healing powers of hope may be the most precious harvest you can glean in the work you do—for yourself and for the youngsters whose lives you touch.[2]

As I reflect on that week, I am mindful how many young people and families are still recovering from the devastating impact of COVID-19 lockdowns, and the disruption to their lifestyles.

How will you interact with the young people whose paths you cross? Start by encouraging them to share their story if they are comfortable doing so.

What messages of hope will you share?

---

2. Henderson, *Resiliency in Action*.

WEEK 33

Practical Strategies to Support Youth from High-Risk Environments

Let your actions speak louder than your words.

> Kids don't need independence, they need interdependence. People are homeless because they have no functioning human relationships in their lives. Who in this society can live independently? All human beings want to belong somewhere.
> —Pat O'Brien, Founder of You Gotta Believe Program for older foster teens in New York

Were you abused as a young person? Do you know someone who was abused as a young person?

Having been an educator for over forty years, I crossed paths with young people who had been physically or emotionally abused, and was often in awe of their resiliency as they worked through life challenges.

I read a deeply disturbing true story by Carrie Bailee, born and raised in Canada, and the trauma she underwent as a child and even as a young adult. *Flying On Broken Wings* is not for the faint-hearted, as Carrie shares the raw brutality of her experiences mostly at the hands of her father.

Yet what struck me as I read this book, was how Carrie found mentors to guide her through much of her adolescent life after she had finally run away from home. She ended up at the home of a single mum with experience working with troubled teens, many of whom were children off the streets.

Tami responded to Carrie's emotional and psychological needs. Carrie writes:

> Tami and I had many conversations during the five years I would float in and out of her life. She would always go to great lengths to assure me that she loved me unconditionally and, no matter what I told her, the love would never change.[1]

Clearly Tami, through the great skill of empathetic listening, displayed exceptional mentoring skills in the life of a broken young woman. Tami's efforts, along with those of other professionals, helped Carrie—an incredibly resilient young woman—on her journey to healing.

Research suggests that some of the more common key characteristics of young people from high-risk environments would include:

- a history of antisocial behavior from an early age (for example, extensive defiance; socially aggressive behavior; substance abuse; theft; cheating; violence, or inappropriate sexual behavior);
- antisocial attitudes, values, and beliefs;
- antisocial associates;
- relationship problems with family, extended family, teachers, peers, and authority figures (for example, indifference, poor social skills, not feeling cared for or valued);
- a difficult temperament (for example, aggressive, callous, impulsive, egocentric);
- problems and low levels of achievement in school, work, or leisure activities;
- early and current family or extended family conditions, including low levels of affection, cohesiveness, or monitoring problems at home which can relate to substance-dependent parents, parents who are either criminal offenders or are incarcerated, foster care, divorced or separated parents, socially disadvantaged families, high levels of stress, or parental depression;
- early and prolonged experience of unemployment.

---

1. Bailee, *Flying on Broken Wings*.

Antisocial behavior can lead to social failure, which may in turn produce a depressed mood. Rejection from peers, family, or extended family problems, and academic difficulties contribute to the onset of depression among boys in particular.

Parenting behavior contributes significantly to the development of a young person's self-esteem. A young person's non-compliance and antisocial behavior are related to low self-esteem.

15 PRACTICAL STRATEGIES TO SUPPORT YOUTH FROM HIGH-RISK ENVIRONMENTS

Mentors have the opportunity to play a significant role in encouraging mentees to believe in themselves, identifying their mentees' resilient qualities, and offering them guidance on how to control their own futures. Mentors recognize that in many cases the task can be tough and challenging, requiring persistence.

If the mentor has assistance from program staff, practical support to mentees may include any number of the following:

1. Advocate some form of ongoing education or skills training, perhaps even undertaking some tutoring, or computer-based instruction to facilitate learning.
2. Assist those wanting to further their education, who often feel overwhelmed by the range of choices of subjects and courses, and by the task of balancing their studies with social activities, sport, and work.
3. Advocate work experience and work ethics training so that mentees can build work histories, and a sense of themselves as workers, as well as earn a living wage.
4. Arrange or run group activities and workshops to promote a positive peer culture, and to help mentees develop life skills.
5. Help to set up financial incentives (linked to the specific mentoring program where relevant), which might include access to financial assistance if needed, to help mentees to save, plan, and believe in their future.
6. Provide intensive emotional support and practical guidance at every step of the way in each mentee's transition time, and have fun together.

PRACTICAL STRATEGIES TO SUPPORT YOUTH

7. Take on a variety of mentoring roles during each mentee's transition time. For example, you may need to be a coach, cheerleader, surrogate parent, advocate, teacher, friend, or mentor who "hangs in" there with your mentee, never giving up on them, no matter how far they have strayed (indeed, the time when mentees stray is the time when they most need mentors and program staff).

8. Promote development activities to learn more about health, alcohol and drug abuse, sexual activities, family planning, arts, career, and education planning.

9. Encourage mentees to become involved in community service activities aimed at improving conditions in their communities.

10. Provide a consistent, reinforcing environment for mentoring and encouraging mentees.

11. Provide a clear structure and limits with well-specified consequences that can be delivered in a teaching- or coaching-oriented way.

12. Closely supervise the mentee's whereabouts (where applicable).

13. Involve mentees in planning for their support and activities.

14. Sensitively and empathetically discourage mentees from associating with peers who have problems (especially conduct-related problems), and help mentees develop skills that will assist them in relationships with positive peers.

Quite a few of these areas of practical support were given to Carrie during the time she spent with Tami, so it's no surprise they formed a meaningful relationship over a number of years.

When we mentor young people, we are likely to encounter a variety of challenges. Eleanor Roosevelt offers words of wisdom: "to handle yourself, use your head; to handle others, use your heart."

Do you have any experiences working with students from high-risk environments to share with others? What worked? What did not work?

WEEK 34

Two Key Words that Cost Us Nothing to Say, Yet Can Be Life-Changing

Attitude is everything. Avoid negativity at all costs.

How many times a day do we pause and say "thank you" to someone who has assisted us in some way?

In the Week 12 musing, I shared my interaction with Dave, my history teacher at school. He had hauled me aside one day and told me that, unless I did some work, I was likely to fail. Sport was more important to me than academic studies. I took up Dave's challenge, gained my best grade in history, and became a history teacher.

Dave later invited me to become a student "stooge" in the boarding house he ran at the school. In return for doing some duties, I received free board and lodging. I jumped at the opportunity and, during the next three years, Dave mentored me. His teaching methods were way ahead of the norm. I was like a sponge as he shared with me, even allowing me to teach some of his younger classes.

Many years later I wrote to Dave to thank him for being such a huge influence in my life. He responded and said that, had he been sitting down when he read my note, he might have fallen off the chair!

Some years later, Dave was dying of cancer. I was living in another country, so I sent a note to his daughter to thank him again. He received the message shortly before he died, and his daughter said that there had been a visible and positive change in his demeanor when she shared that simple message.

Two key words: "thank you."

Can you remember the last time you said "thank you" to someone who has positively impacted your life in a significant way? It's never too late to do so.

I have immense gratitude for the people who moved alongside me, and guided me in a variety of ways when I entered the workforce during difficult and challenging economic and political times.

There were so many unknowns—what was the future looking like? How do I budget? Who can I trust? Who do I approach for guidance? Am I really up for this job?

> When we get discouraged in our work with people it is important to draw back and remind ourselves that there is no more noble occupation in the world than to assist another human being, to help someone else succeed.
> —Alan Loy McGinnis

Can you remember the people who influenced you the most when you joined the workforce? How does the workplace today differ from when you entered it for the first time? How would you motivate and encourage a young adult to join your team in their first career move?

These are interesting questions to consider. They are questions I have been reflecting upon as I think about how the COVID-19 pandemic has impacted economic development, and shattered the dreams of many young people.

Neuroscience researchers continually remind us that young people's brains are only fully developed when they are in their mid-twenties. This highlights the importance of empathetic employers guiding and navigating new young employees entering the workforce for the first time.

I spent some time researching employer and employee relationships, exploring what social researchers say, and reading general articles in which employers share their experiences working with youth.

I have observed over the years how the advent of technology has changed the mindset of young employees. In some cases, I saw youth unafraid to be creative and innovative. In other situations, I observed young people unable to empathize with others, severely lacking teamwork skills, and often with questionable social and management of time skills.

I saw others who took life so seriously, were unable to laugh at themselves, and whose perfectionist attitude led to heightened stress levels. I observed others who lacked a healthy and balanced lifestyle, which had a negative effect on their output.

I noted others who had no idea how to cope with the challenges of the workplace, and either left the workforce voluntarily, or were asked to move on.

14 TOP MOTIVATORS FOR EMPLOYERS OF YOUNG ADULTS

Here are fourteen top motivators for employers of young people to reflect on, always remembering that every employee is unique, different, and brings their personal life story to the work place.

1. They value flexibility in terms of hours of work.
2. Offer access to state-of-the art training opportunities which are preferably experiential rather than totally online learning. They often require "soft skills" training to build meaningful relationships with other employees, customers, or clients—presentation, management, management of time, communication, and team-building skills.
3. Encourage mentoring opportunities, whereby a wise guide moves alongside them, is non-judgmental and empathetic, and encourages them to chase their dreams, and reach their potential.
4. Mentoring is a great vehicle for values sharing and knowledge transfer. Young people listen to and observe everything going on around them, even when one thinks this is not the case.
5. They respond positively to inspiring and motivational leadership from authentic and trustworthy leaders.
6. Recognition and reward—genuinely affirm these young people when they complete a task well, most especially commenting on their efforts.
7. Most young people enjoy the challenge of understanding cutting-edge technology. Explore ways you can use their skills to coach other colleagues, as this will create a superb collaborative team.
8. They appreciate honest, regular, and constructive feedback, though the timing of this feedback is also important in their personal development journey.

9. Make sure that they have a clear understanding of their role in the big picture. They want meaning and purpose in their lives.
10. Share messages of hope and coach them how to envision the future. Discuss with them how "instant gratification" and "entitlement" attitudes will not assist their personal growth; that failure occurs, and the key is *how* they learn from failure; that *every* choice they make will have a consequence of some sort.
11. Make sure you offer an inclusive, participative, non-threatening team environment in which they feel able to contribute, and their ideas and opinions are valued. Indeed, someone once commented that if you want to watch a person grow several inches in stature before your eyes, just praise them in public.
12. Develop an environment which acknowledges their preferred style of learning: social, collaborative, interactive, and fun.
13. Encourage them to live a healthy and balanced lifestyle.

> Sedentary children suffer from high rates of obesity and all its associated health issues and risks, which is why it's important to develop a healthy and active lifestyle at an early age.[1]
> —Hector Garcia and Francesc Miralles

14. Encourage them to stay informed about the dangers of substance abuse, even to connect with others who are finding their way.

As the global community recovers from the impact of COVID-19, the creative, innovative, and entrepreneurial spirits of our youth can be encouraged and rewarded.

Employers can play a significant role in transforming many of these young lives who have been battered by the negative impact of lockdowns. Their self-confidence has been dented, and they have felt unable to pursue their dreams because of the pandemic's impact on their lives, perhaps also on their family's life and circumstances.

Maybe you have a story to share of how an employer guided you at a critical time in your life? There are many young people keen to hear you share your experiences.

To whom can you say those two key words: "thank you"?

---

1. Garcia and Miralles, *Ikigai*.

WEEK 35

How to Encourage Others to Achieve Greatness

Let your curiosity guide you into discovering new paths.

How important are your face-to-face relationships to you? How often do you reach out and connect with someone who would value your non-judgmental support and guidance?

I had the privilege of sharing mentoring thoughts with a relatively new mentoring program serving the area in which I used to live, so I had a sound knowledge of the challenges the mentors were facing from a discussion I had with the program coordinator prior to the meeting.

I listened to the experiences of four new mentors who had been mentoring their mentees for a couple of months. The mentees were vulnerable young people on a journey through their confusing adolescent years.

As the mentors shared, what became abundantly clear was that when a young person has a significant adult in their lives who reaches out, cares, and speaks to their potential, they are keen to connect.

These face-to-face relationships will thrive and, hopefully, one day those young people will reach out to other young people looking for a significant adult in their lives.

10 STRATEGIES FOR EFFECTIVE MENTORING

After I had shared a couple of mentoring stories with the mentors, I presented them with a summary of proven tips and strategies they could reflect on in their efforts to make a difference in these young people's lives. Indeed, these strategies could be adapted when a mentor moves alongside anyone of any age with whom they interact.

These strategies are the results of years of research, and a collation of key characteristics of effective mentors gathered from the work of respected global mentoring experts and leaders.

They can also become part of student peer mentor or peer support programs, or to enhance leadership training at any level.

1. *Do not quit!* A mentoring relationship can sometimes stumble and stall. Persevere.
2. *Be genuine.* Trust, empathy, and respect are solid foundations on which a mentoring relationship is built.
3. *Be non-judgmental.* Unconditional love and care give the mentoring relationship a greater chance of succeeding.
4. *Turn up and stay in touch.* Regular interaction with your mentee enhances the possibility of a positive connection. Mentors drive the relationship in the early months, no matter the age of the mentee; be punctual for every meeting you plan with your mentee.
5. *Don't expect to have all the answers.* Mentors are human beings who are not expected to be perfect, so seek support from other mentors and program staff (as applicable).
6. *Be a valuable resource.* Mentors are valued as key resources by mentees, especially when they link their mentees to personal networks.
7. *Be realistic about the relationship.* Mentors are expected to be a friend, advocate, and guide, not a savior, rescuer, or someone offering quick-fix solutions to complex problems.
8. *Listen.* Effective communication techniques produce mentoring from the heart.
9. *Celebrate the small victories.* Be a positive cheerleader in your mentee's life, helping them to achieve realistic goals, and look for every opportunity to acknowledge their *effort*, rather than focus on performance.

10. *Have clear boundaries and expectations.* Communicate and negotiate ground rules with your mentee at the outset, and revisit these as often as necessary during the mentoring journey.

> Life is a song—sing it.
> Life is a game—play it.
> Life is a challenge—meet it.
> Life is a dream—realize it.
> Life is a sacrifice—offer it.
> Life is love—enjoy it.
> —Sai Baba

Have you any additional tips from your life experiences to pass on to those mentoring young people?

WEEK 36

The Ultimate 17 Point Personal Growth Kit

Let your laughter be contagious, no matter what your circumstances.

How easy do you find it to make friends or encourage others? Why do you value the friends you currently have? How prepared are you to encourage others?

Are you a solutions-focused person? Or, do you share more feelings of doom and gloom than expressions of joy and happiness—what is possible with a positive attitude?

Or, do you feel full of self-pity, or overwhelmed at times, especially during this season of many conflicting global challenges?

Some years ago, I came across a *Survival Kit for Everybody Living*. I have unsuccessfully searched to find the developer of the Survival Kit which contains many great tips and ideas to share with others.

It got me thinking about mentoring, or guiding our youth as their brains are still developing to pursue their goals and dreams.

I borrowed five of those nine contents of the Survival Kit, adapted some of them, and added another ten to create a *17 Point Personal Growth Kit*.

17 POINT PERSONAL GROWTH KIT

A mentor could grab a paper bag, put all these items in the bag, which they present to their mentee (of any age in reality), and explain what each item represents. Alternatively, you could select five or ten items from the list. Some fascinating discussions could occur.

The mentee will have in their possession seventeen reminders they can carry through life and share with others—maybe one day with their own mentees—as they strive to reach their potential.

This is a non-threatening activity which could be life-changing for a mentee seeking meaning and purpose in their lives, and wanting to feel valued and respected.

1. *Toothpick*: A reminder to pick out the good qualities in others.
2. *Rubber band*: A reminder to be flexible. Things might not always go the way you want, but it will work out.
3. *Band Aid*: A reminder to heal hurt feelings—yours or someone else's. It's your choice.
4. *Pencil*: A reminder to list at least three blessings—three things to be thankful for—every day.
5. *Eraser*: A reminder that everyone makes mistakes, and it's okay—try and learn one important life lesson from every mistake, and you'll develop a positive mindset. There *is* a solution to every problem.
6. *Small glue stick*: A reminder to stick with it, persist, and you can accomplish anything.
7. *Key ring*: A reminder that your attitude will determine the choices you make as you shape your future. *You* alone hold the key to your future. Every choice has a consequence.
8. *Two linked paper clips*: A reminder to stay connected with friends and family—people you trust. Value significant relationships and build positive networks of support.
9. *Staples*: A reminder of the importance of a staple diet to give you the necessary energy each day to live a healthy and balanced lifestyle.
10. *Shoelace*: A reminder to undertake regular exercise for healthy living, and positive brain development.

11. *Small ruler:* A reminder to set realistic, achievable, and measurable personal best goals to be completed within a certain timeframe.

12. *Colored crayon:* A reminder that everyone is a person of value and beauty on the inside and outside, and will appreciate a hug (where appropriate) to brighten their day.

13. *Pencil sharpener:* A reminder never to become complacent; to keep sharpening your skills; to be a lifelong learner; teachable, and coachable.

14. *Smiley face fridge magnet:* A reminder never to take yourself too seriously, and to develop the ability to laugh at yourself.

15. *Small tea leaf strainer (or something similar):* A reminder of the importance of between eight and nine hours sleep every night to allow your body to rest and your brain to process what is and is not important—and to file these in the correct places—from the day's experiences. Healthy mind, healthy body.

16. *Small bouncing ball:* A reminder that you have many strengths and are resilient, so you *can* bounce back from any adversity.

17. *Small mirror:* A reminder to take time out each day to reflect on your day and to remember that you are lovable and capable—a beautiful person on the inside and outside (your choice). Write on the back: "Have I done my best today?" Reflect on this question every day. If you answer "yes," brilliant—well done! If you answer "no," make a note of the area or skill to keep working on to reach your full potential. This is learning for life.

Maybe you can think of other items with key messages to add to the Personal Growth Kit?

WEEK 37

Thoughts on Becoming a Positive Influencer

Live life by your own expectations, and make every day an adventure.

How positively do you influence those around you?

It takes wisdom, maturity, and humility to ask for help. And, it's a sign of strength, not weakness. That's hard to come to terms with, for those of us who take pride in our ability to "do it all."

As a leader, it's easy to overestimate your own importance and competence.

We are created to be interdependent, not independent.

When you try to be "all things to all people," you end up frustrated. You're not called to do it all, but to get it done through others. That's what leadership is about.

When people feel "used" they begin to drop out, but when they feel appreciated, they'll follow you anywhere.

President Theodore Roosevelt once said, "The best executive is the one who has the sense enough to pick good men [women] to do what he [she] wants done, and self-restraint to keep from meddling with them while they do it." Bottom line: unless you learn to delegate, your leadership will deteriorate, and your vision will stagnate.

FIVE CHARACTERISTICS OF GOOD AND EFFECTIVE LEADERS

Here are five common characteristics of good and effective leaders, which I have collated from my research over the years. Good and effective leaders:

1. *are consistent.* They set an example by walking the walk so everyone knows that what's heard at the bottom is practiced at the top.
2. *voice their appreciation*, realizing that people need to know they're an important part of the team, and the vision.
3. *always respectfully listen to suggestions, opinions, concerns and ideas.* They don't pre-judge, and they're not dismissive. Author Betty Bender said, "It's a mistake to surround yourself only with people just like you. Throw off that warm comforter and replace it with a crazy quilt of different and imaginative people. Then watch the ideas erupt!"
4. *don't see people as statistics.* Businesswoman, Mary Kay Ash said, "P&L doesn't mean 'profit and loss'—it means 'people and love.'"
5. *explain why they like things done a specific way.* It lessens mistakes, and the resentment that can stem from feeling "ordered around." Statesman Clarence Francis said: "You can buy a man's time and physical presence at a certain place . . . But you can't buy enthusiasm, initiative, loyalty, and the devotion of hearts, minds, and souls. You have to earn these things."

When you crave acceptance and approval, you end up being controlled by those you're supposed to lead.

Afraid of causing upheaval in the ranks, insecure leaders agonize over decisions and assume responsibility for other people's emotional reactions. They don't realize that when you're doing what you should be doing and others don't agree, that's their problem, unless you make it yours.

A mature leader deals with disappointment and keeps a good attitude; they're willing to face the music even when they don't like the tune.

The truth is, some people won't like hearing the word "no" regardless of how old they are. We all need to hear the word "no" from time to time, otherwise we'll never be happy with anything other than getting our own way—and that means getting nowhere, or getting into trouble.

Correct people when they're wrong, rebuke them when they're stubborn, encourage them when they struggle, be patient as they learn to grow, and make sure your instructions are clear and understandable. That's what good leaders do—and the only way they learn it is by doing it.

There are many talented leaders who never become effective. Why? Because they're more interested in themselves than in those they lead. What's interesting, however, is that once they go through the school of hard knocks, they become sensitized to other people's needs.

Good leaders don't wait for that to happen. They realize that ideas are a dime a dozen, but people who can implement them are priceless.

Legendary American football coach Bear Bryant used to say, "I'm just a plough-hand from Arkansas, but I've learned to hold a team together. How to lift some men up, how to calm others down, until finally they've got one heartbeat together. There are just three things I'd ever say: If something goes bad, I did it. If it goes semi-good, we did it. If anything goes really well, then you did it."

When you have the gift of leadership, you'll also be approachable. You won't fly off the handle, you won't let minor problems poison your outlook, and you'll sandwich every slice of criticism between two layers of praise.

Author Robert Louis Stevenson said, "Keep your fears to yourself, but share your courage with others."

There are people who knock the heart out of you, and people who put it back in. The latter is the kind of leader each of us can aspire to become, one who actively models the spirit of mentoring.

What kind of leader and mentor are you? How positively are you influencing others?

WEEK 38

My Relationships Matter to Me

Plant seeds today even if there was no tomorrow.

Which relationships mean the most to you? Why this choice, or these choices?

Did you have any significant relationships with adults, including your parents, during your youth? What made those relationships special?

Are you struggling with *any* relationships at the moment?

Here are some key qualities which will assist anyone wanting to move alongside another person and encourage them to reach their potential. Some of the content has been shared in other musings in this book. Think of the word: *RELATIONSHIPS*. Repetition is deliberate.

- Respect: respect both the other person and yourself as unique beings of great self-worth with a positive self-image. Acknowledge their right to make choices. Help them appreciate how *every* choice has a consequence.

- Empathy: do your best to place yourself in the shoes of the other person in order to understand them better, a key quality of emotional intelligence to model to those we move alongside. The digital age has caused many of our youth (and others) to struggle to interpret tone of voice, body language, and facial features.

*L*isten: often those we move alongside feel that they are not being heard, and that their opinions and ideas are neither respected nor valued. Make sure you hear what they say, as well as what they might not be saying. Reflect back to them what you believe they have shared as you model effective communication strategies. You will create a quicker connection with the other person.

*A*ttitude: model how a positive attitude can impact our choices when we encourage others to step out of their comfort zone, and risk possible failure. This well-known saying is worth sharing: "Your attitude will determine how high and far you fly (your altitude)." A positive attitude leads to the growth of a positive mindset. Help others to appreciate that they alone are responsible for the attitude they choose.

*T*eamwork: guide others to become people of positive influence, able to work in teams composed of a variety of cultures, and to tolerate and respect the ideas and opinions of others. Coach them how to *positively* resolve conflicts which will inevitably arise as team members share ideas and opinions, and how to have fun. Teach them the importance of laughing at themselves, and not taking life too seriously.

*I*nnovative: the world of work requires innovative and creative thinking. Encourage those you move alongside to step out of their comfort zone, risk and learn from failure, and never to fear failure as they dare greatly. Identify their strengths and name them.

*O*pen-minded: be that wise guide on the side. Accept others as they are. Remain objective—able to look at all sides of an argument or situation as you encourage another person to interact positively with others, and learn to cope with new situations. Coach them how to negotiate with others in a respectful manner.

*N*urture: create a supportive environment in which the other person feels cared for, affirmed, and encouraged. Commit to the other person, believe in them, be accessible to them, an effective listener, and a consistent presence in their lives.

*S*ervice: the relationship is about encouraging others—it's about giving of yourself without expecting any reward. Focus on the specific needs and issues of the other person, and not on trying to push your agenda. Share with others the importance of giving back to their community.

*H*umility: linked to service is the need to model humility at all times, coaching others how to be gracious in defeat, and modeling how to look for the good in others to create positive communities.

*I*nspire: Inspire and motivate others to become the best people they can be. Coach them how to set realistic, achievable, and measurable goals. They *can* reach their potential as they come to believe in their own self-worth, and acknowledge that they usually have control over things that happen to them, and how they choose to react.

*P*ersist: never stop supporting a person you move alongside. Young people, especially, are on a journey through one of the most confusing periods of their lives, searching for meaning and purpose, and will value the significant adult who says: "I believe in you," or "Come on, we can do this together."

*S*incerity: be authentic at all times. That is, be aware of your innermost thoughts and feelings, accept them and, when appropriate, share them responsibly (self-expression); know yourself (self-awareness), and accept yourself (self-acceptance).

When you focus on developing these key qualities, they guide those you move alongside to develop resiliency, and a positive growth mindset.

> In order for children to respond with resilience, they must first learn the connection between their thoughts and their feelings and behaviors. It is as important for children as it is for you [mentor, parent], because children have as many adversities in their lives as adults do.
> —Karen Reivich and Andrew Shatte[1]

There is that wonderful moment when, many years after I have mentored a student, our paths cross, and I receive feedback about something I did or shared without knowing how it impacted that young life at the time.

I am left humbled when I receive a comment such as this, written by Ross:

> It is very nice to be in touch. I have always wanted to thank you for the role you played in my life at [school]. I remember our history lessons with pleasure, but mainly chats and a Coke after our weekly squash games. It made a big difference to me that you showed me that care and interest. I have appreciated that for thirty

---

1. Reivich and Shatte, *The Resilience Factor*, 270.

years, and think of you often. It is with you that I recall having my first conversation with anyone about wanting to become a [career choice] . . . It has gone well for me, but the first step was with you, and our discussions of why I lost matches from 2–0 up were my first [career] experiences. Mentoring Matters is a wonderful project that I am sure has given you the opportunity to affect many lives in the way you influenced mine.[2]

Do you have a story to share about how you have positively moved alongside and nurtured someone to reach their full potential?

2. Cox, *Mentoring Minutes*, 78–79

WEEK 39

Proven Goal-Setting Tips: My Personal Experience

Have a clear vision of mind. Never lose your sense of humor.

Do you set your personal best goals? How often do you give up on them?

Does the experience feel like you are walking along a rocky path shrouded in mist sometimes—so much unknown?

Did you set goals when you were a teenager? Did you ever have someone who helped you?

If you did set goals, how effective was the process you followed? Did you achieve your goals, or did you quit? Did you always feel you were reaching your potential?

I have been a goal-setter for most of my life. My goals motivated and inspired me to stay focused, and to stand up to negative peer pressure on occasions.

While I might not have achieved all my goals, I learnt much about myself through the process—and continue to do so—and enjoyed that amazing feeling when I managed to achieve a specific goal, be it academic, sport, relational, or pursuing a hobby, or some other activity.

What did I learn from the experience?

Well, the truth is that I never stop learning. Although now retired, I still set annual goals, and break these down into monthly goals, because I want to lead *a healthy and balanced lifestyle and enjoy a fulfilling life*.

The work I have done over the years as a teacher, sport coach, and mentor of teenagers *always* involves goal-setting. I have learnt that, when a young person starts achieving their personal best goals, they begin to find meaning and purpose in their lives, and they are more motivated and happier, outcomes supported by adolescent brain research.

20 STRATEGIES AND TIPS TO ACHIEVE GOALS

These twenty random strategies and tips, which have guided my thinking, can be adapted by mentors to the particular community in which they are working. Remember, goal-setting comes, for the most part, *after* you have established a connection with your mentee, and some feelings of mutual trust exist, a process that could take time. Much will depend on the background and current circumstances of your mentee.

1. Have a clear picture (your personal photograph) of what you want to achieve.
2. Make sure the goal you are working towards is something *you* really want to attain.
3. Always write your goal as a positive visualization statement.
4. Always write out your goal in complete detail.
5. Start the goal-setting process with small, specific, measurable and easily achievable action steps (short-term goals), and then begin to stretch yourself a little more as your self-confidence increases. Ensure that every goal has a clear deadline.
6. Make a list of anticipated obstacles, and see how many can be converted into positive opportunities—is there someone you trust who can help you with this?
7. Identify all the skills, information, knowledge, resources and help from people and organizations that you will need to achieve your goals.
8. Always ensure that you have a clear plan of action in place.

9. Remember that goals change as you mature. You should review them regularly, adjust them when and where necessary, or reframe them, thus reflecting the growth in your personality, your life changes, your priority changes, and new opportunities.

10. Don't let goal-setting become your master—goals must bring you real pleasure, satisfaction, and a sense of achievement. If this is not happening, revisit them.

11. Personal factors such as tiredness, other commitments, and the need for rest, as examples, should be taken into account when you set your goals.

12. Don't set too many goals at any one time.

> We often think that combining tasks will save us time, but scientific evidence shows that it has the opposite effect. Even those who claim to be good at multitasking are not very productive. In fact, they are some of the least productive people.
> —Hector Garcia and Francesc Miralles[1]

> Multitasking works *against* your brain. Every time you shift your attention between tasks, you deplete your neural resources and lose focus. In fact, research shows that it takes almost thirty minutes to refocus your attention completely after it has been diverted. This makes you not only less creative and imaginative, but also less productive, and it decreases the quality of the work or enjoyment of whatever—or *whomever*—you're focusing on.
> —Asheesh Advani[2]

13. Be consistent and have the courage to act and take non-life-threatening risks.

14. Set challenging goals that require energy and self-discipline to achieve.

15. Reward your progress towards the achievement of your goal—celebrate *every* small step.

16. Focus on your goals on a daily basis (consider placing your goals in a video which you can often refer to, perhaps share with someone you trust, or place them in a diary, or on your mobile phone).

---

1. Garcia and Miralles, *Ikigai*.
2. Advani and Goldsmith, *Modern Achievement*.

17. Consider setting your goals after you have discussed management of time with someone you trust, remembering that *you* manage your own time.
18. Ensure that your goals are aligned to your values, your mission, and your purpose in life.
19. Rid yourself of the negative factors—including the negative people—in your life, as best as you can.
20. Use your failures as learning curves for planning future successes.

Always seek to make the setting of personal best goals a fun and enjoyable aspect of the mentoring journey.

How are you doing with your goals? Do you have a goal-getting story to share with a young person?

WEEK 40

Exploring the Connection between Mentoring and Jigsaw Puzzles

Stay close to your pencil and dream, for life's greatest accomplishments start off with them.

When last did you complete a jigsaw puzzle? Or do you prefer crossword puzzles, or Sudoku, and those types of mind games?

I completed a jigsaw puzzle recently. It took me about three days, though I was doing it at various times of the day and night, as I don't enjoy becoming too intense about it.

I particularly enjoy the 1000 pieces *Wasgij* puzzles, where one doesn't know the final picture, and has to use one's imagination, creativity, and develop strategies to work out the best way forward.

In many ways this activity reminded me of some of the challenges of a mentoring journey. Let me explain, though only after we consider how completing puzzles might be benefitting the brain.

Some years ago, I started doing jigsaw puzzles as a friend of mine suggested they were a great way of keeping the brain sharp, especially as one aged.

Dr Shen-Li Lee, author of *Brainchild: Secrets to unlocking your child's potential*[1], and creator of a parenting website *figure 8.net*, shared some

---

1. Lee, *Brainchild*.

research she undertook about jigsaw puzzles, and the positive impact on the brain.

From her research, which she states can't be scientifically proven, she collated some of her findings about the benefits of solving jigsaw puzzles:

- enhances visual perception;
- hones coordination;
- improves memory;
- develops critical thinking;
- increases dopamine production in the brain;
- heightens creativity;
- stimulates the whole brain.

If all these bullet points were proven to be scientifically true, it would justify the number of hours I spend wrapped up in trying to solve the picture puzzle.

A great mentoring tip appears in this information: encourage your mentee to do puzzles to keep developing their brain.

Better still, if you can complete a puzzle together, imagine the conversations and teamwork skills that could occur, and the fun that would be enjoyed by the two of you—maybe some frustrations too.

We probably have different strategies we use when we complete puzzles, and that's why it is like mentoring in some ways, especially with regard to the *Wasgij* puzzles. When we enter a mentoring relationship, we have absolutely no idea what the end result is going to be.

With the puzzle, we study the initial picture, and then the clues that are often provided. Similarly, in a mentoring relationship, we observe two strangers brought together seeking common ground in an initial, fairly superficial conversation. "Tell me about your family." "Do you play sport or a music instrument?" "Where do you live?" "How long have you lived there?" "How many hobbies do you have?"

Just as I study the clues before I begin the puzzle, so in the mentoring relationship I'll seek common ground, or similar interests when I meet my mentee for the first time. My goal is to *connect* with my mentee.

I ask non-threatening or non-intrusive questions, which also allow me to respond, be vulnerable and, hopefully, through sharing some of my story, encourage my mentee to start sharing their thoughts and opinions.

I look for the border pieces, the frame of the puzzle, which helps me see some structure to the puzzle. Similarly, as a mentor, I negotiate boundaries in place early on to ensure that my mentee feels safe, secure, and comfortable in this developmental relationship.

When I work on the jigsaw puzzle and sort out the pieces, I look for colors, faces, body parts, and words, or letters, and place these in a separate area; maybe there are certain building pieces, items of clothing, for example, which I can detect.

I am planning and organizing the pieces, also setting small goals as I identify the different pieces. While my ultimate goal is to complete the puzzle, I need to achieve this with small action steps—the different characters and shapes I separate out early on.

The mentor aims to see the mentee enjoy a fun, self-empowering journey, hence the focus as early as possible on setting personal best goals, management of time, planning, and organizing. Together, as with the puzzle, strategies are created.

Open-ended questions enrich our mentoring relationship and, just as I try and do with the creator of the puzzle, I attempt to stand in my mentee's shoes to imagine the end picture.

Similarly, as a mentor, I try to encourage my mentee to develop their personal long-term vision. Then we work backwards to the present day, and begin the initial small, doable, and achievable action steps.

After a while my eyes tire and I begin to lose focus on the puzzle, at times feeling frustrated as my progress is so slow. I stand up and move away, often for a few hours, during which time I still hold a vague picture of what I think the puzzle will look like once completed.

As a mentor, I head off after our mentoring time and have a chance to reflect, sometimes making some notes to remind me of a conversation we have had.

When I meet my mentee the next time, with fresh eyes, just as with the puzzle, I might suddenly see some pieces coming together. My mentee might share something, and, as though a missing link has been found, I gather a greater perspective about my mentee.

This mentoring journey, like the puzzle, takes time to develop, and often has unpredictable turns. Perseverance is not only important when I complete puzzles, but also during the mentoring journey.

We bring our unique gifts and talents to the mentoring relationship and, over time, our relationship is shaped and refined, our respective strengths acknowledged, and we work at ways to support one another. Most of the time the adult mentor is the main source of encouragement to the younger mentee.

As with the frustrations of not fitting pieces to the puzzle at different times, so the mentoring relationship can be frustrating, depending on the mood and feelings of the mentee when we meet. I need patience—that quality of endurance that can reach breaking point and not break—and to remember one golden rule for the mentoring journey shared years ago by a mentee: "Don't quit on your mentee."

When I complete the puzzle, I enjoy a wonderful feeling of satisfaction. There is a positive dopamine release in my brain as I study the final picture, always marveling at the ingenuity of the creator of the puzzle. I leave it out overnight, and stand proudly looking at it again the next morning before I break it up, box it, and usually pass it on to a friend.

We have no idea how short or long our mentoring relationship will last. What's important is to celebrate every small goal achieved, as that boosts the self-empowering journey of the mentee, and builds self-belief and self-confidence.

I am tempted to find another puzzle now that I am in the groove, but I know the importance of a balanced and healthy lifestyle, so I must wait awhile, and be reminded of the importance of discussing what a healthy and balanced lifestyle means to my adolescent mentee.

Do you attempt jigsaw puzzles, or any other puzzles? What strategies can you share with mentees?

WEEK 41

Mentoring Lessons from the Olympic Games

Be accurate in what you do. It makes all the difference in the world.

Have you watched any Olympic Games events? Was there a particular moment or event highlight for you? Have you thought about ways to use the Olympic Games to motivate and inspire a young person to reach their potential?

I love most sports, played plenty of sport when I was younger—with differing levels of success—and then coached for over thirty years.

However, I also appreciate that many people do not enjoy sport, and probably do not watch the Olympics. Perhaps they have seen glimpses of the opening ceremony on their news channel?

That provides an opportunity to discuss the effective use of innovative and creative gifts with others, young people especially.

Of course, there are the moving scenes of an Olympian achieving a medal, and being overcome with emotion in that moment of realizing that something they have been working towards for twenty years has been achieved.

There are many others who achieve a "personal best," and the sheer satisfaction and enjoyment as they attain this goal is celebrated with such fervor, even if there was no medal gained.

And then there are others who stumble and fall, crash out of an event for which they have trained so hard, and for so long, or fall short by one hundredth of a second, for example, from attaining a medal.

Perhaps they are members of a team, and a team mate has stumbled and fallen, robbing them of a chance to display their talents on the Olympic stage.

There will be a multitude of emotions experienced at an Olympic Games.

I wonder how many dreams were shattered? How do those Olympians work through their experience?

Spare a thought, too, for those who have withdrawn from the Olympics because they picked up an illness, or a virus, or suffered an injury—all that training, hard work, and sacrifice for what?

If the young person you are guiding to reach their potential has watched any aspect of the Olympics, you can have discussions about the life lessons one can take from preparing and participating in an Olympic Games: setting personal best goals; strategies for handling setbacks; responding to inner and outer conflicts; communicating effectively with others in a variety of situations, and the importance of living a healthy and balanced lifestyle.

I have listened to some of the interviews with Olympians, and wondered how many of them are actually living a healthy and balanced lifestyle in the "real world?" And then I read a headline about how the Olympians need to be supported once the Olympics is over and they return to the "real world."

It is important to share with youth the reminder that:

> No one will stand on a winner's podium who has not spent years practicing, learning, and pressing through pain barriers to realize their dream. Not a single athlete will have made it alone without the help of a team, a trainer, supporters, and the confidence of whose who believed in them.[1]

Most participants acknowledge this when they speak to the media. *Positive relationships* are a key indicator in most Olympian achievements.

The young person we move alongside for a season can also have their "Olympian" moment: selection for a specific team; achieving a significant

---

1. Cox, *99 Musings*, 172.

grade; overcoming a particularly challenging obstacle, or working through a particularly difficult time.

EIGHT MENTORING LESSONS FROM THE OLYMPIC GAMES

We can discuss ways to live a healthy and balanced life with youth—indeed with anyone—and here are eight mentoring lessons from the Olympics Games which can fan that discussion. Think of the word OLYMPICS. Repetition is deliberate.

1. *Organization*—every Olympian sets a realistic, achievable, specific goal which will be measured by their result at the games. However, to achieve this goal they have to follow a plan, or a roadmap of sorts, which they developed with a coach: a training program, diet, events in which to participate as preparation for the games, and people who can support them on this journey. We must be organized and continually evaluate our progress, unafraid to make changes and improvements when necessary.

2. *Leadership*—*every* Olympian becomes a person of influence as they enter the world stage. Others, especially youth, look up to them, and are inspired by them. They regard Olympians as role models, and want to emulate them. Discuss different leadership styles and qualities—empathy, patience, teamwork, loyalty, maintaining a sense of humor, being a peacemaker at times, tolerance, and looking for the best in others—as well as embracing the other seven lessons mentioned in this musing.

3. *Youthful*—it is important for anyone working with youth to remain youthful. What is this young person's story? What are their hopes and dreams? What are their fears? Who influences them the most? We take a positive attitude into our mentoring relationship, including gentleness, compassion, kindness, and tolerance. We coach them when and how to be vulnerable as they share deeper thoughts and experiences.

4. *Motivation*—the mentor's consistent presence, travelling at the pace of the young person, can be transformational in that young life. Ongoing encouragement, no matter how small the step achieved towards the ultimate goal, builds resilience. Explore together the lives of the young

person's hero or heroes, as well as any heroes you have had over the years. Why these people? How are they Olympians? What positive qualities did they possess? You can imagine different scenarios and discuss these with your mentee to prepare them as thoroughly as possible for the challenges ahead.

5. *Perseverance*—there will be a few times when a young person finds the goal-setting process too hard, or they are distracted by other people—often negative peer pressure—or other diversions. They are scared of failure, or to move out of their comfort zone. Every Olympian is likely to have been through such experiences, but they persisted, bounced back, and continued the journey to achieve their goal. Youth need to hear the mentor's voice speaking to the potential they might not be able to see at that moment. Remind them of people like Thomas Edison who refused to think of failure during the thousands of experiments before he successfully developed the light bulb—learn something from every unsuccessful attempt, and keep striving to reach the goal. *Effort* is more important than the eventual outcome in the eyes of an effective mentor. The encouragement from the non-judgmental mentor can transform a young life. The aim is to hear your mentee echo the words of many Olympians: "I gave it my all." "I left everything out there." This is what doing your personal best is about.

6. *Integrity*—focus on being authentic at all times. Coach the young person how to be humble in victory, and gracious in defeat; not to be too hard on themselves; never to cheat; never to be afraid to ask for help, and to have a positive and honest attitude at all times, no matter what the personal cost might be.

7. *Choices*—a great lesson from the Olympics is how Olympians have made choices along the road to the Olympics, even in their individual events at the games: "Should I try this strategy?" "Should we take a calculated risk?" "What if we do this or that?" Share thoughts with youth about the importance of self-discipline, self-control, and always striving to be a positive role model because "people are watching" them. Share a variety of photos of Olympians succeeding, failing, or expressing anger, or frustration. Ask questions like: "What do you think of this behavior?" "How do you think the player's sponsors will feel?" "How do you think their fellow countrymen and women will feel?" "Should there be a more serious consequence than simply

receiving a warning (code violation)? Why, or why not?" "How do you think this sort of behavior could be linked to becoming a professional athlete who earns millions of dollars a year?" "Is he or she a role model you look up to? Why, or why not?" "How do you think that athlete feels with a medal around their neck?" "Would you like to explore this athlete's life journey on the internet?"

8. Success—find success in the small as well as the big achievements, in the very fact of taking that first step to change to become a better person. With success develop selflessness. For example, I recall the story of an athlete at the 2020 Olympics who heard that they would receive a financial payment for their medal achievement. They immediately gave the money to their needy parent. Selflessness inspires others. A mentor who models selflessness must never underestimate how this will impact a young life.

Perhaps you are an Olympian, former Olympian, or know someone who has participated in the Olympics, and has a story to share. Young people are inspired by true stories.

WEEK 42

Reflecting on Life's Meaning and Purpose

Be willing to follow your path even through life's curves.

"Who am I?" "What is the meaning and purpose of my life?"

Anyone who has moved alongside young people will appreciate that these are two of the many questions, albeit *key* questions they ask during their journey to become a young adult.

I was reflecting on a time soon after I retired when I was on my daily beach walk. The tide was low and many people were exercising and enjoying the beauty of the morning; an appropriate time for reflecting about the meaning and purpose of life, especially from a mentoring perspective.

Some of my observations included how unique we are, and how we each walk at our own pace.

Footprints were different shapes, sizes, depths, and angles. Some walkers were barefoot and there were also a variety of dog paw sizes scattered among the footprints.

I spent time looking at the people on the beach:

- some, like me, were walking briskly and with purpose on their own;

- some, mostly older people, also walked with purpose, though were in small groups chatting animatedly—interesting too how there were gender specific groups within the larger group;
- some jogged; others paused to pick up shells, or drank a cup of tea or coffee purchased from a nearby cafe, or brought from home in a special cup; a few carried bottled water;
- a few talked on mobile phones, some gesticulating as they shared a thought, or were deeply absorbed in a conversation (body language was interesting), while a couple of people took photos of the beautiful scene with their phones;
- some paused to chat to friends. These were mostly locals, who I greet with a "hello" and smile most days. They talk about life, local experiences, the weather, or their dogs;
- many were wearing glasses, and hats or caps to protect them from the summer sun;
- some walked with purpose and never greeted me—their choice.

Come to think of it, this daily walk is an amazing experience which I *never* take for granted. The weather is *never* the same. Every wave is *unique*, never to be seen again. As the waves roll up onto the shore, they create different patterns *never* to be repeated, a reminder that every person on the beach that morning was an individual with their own life story.

Has their life been an amazing adventure, or do they regard their life experiences as fairly ordinary?

Have they ever suffered the disappointment of losing a job, or a significant business deal, or a loved one unexpectedly, or experienced a broken relationship?

How many countries have they lived in during their lives?

What careers have these people experienced?

Have they possibly enjoyed the highs and lows of taking calculated, innovative and creative risks embraced by an entrepreneurial spirit? What were the results?

Are any of them a victim of abuse?

Are any of them abusers, or people with bullying tendencies?

Do any have alcohol, drug, or some other mental health issues they are grappling with—perhaps some antisocial behaviors?

So many questions.

I wonder how they would respond if I asked them: "What is the most important issue you are dealing with today?"

Anyone I mentor brings their personal story to our relationship. I do my best to empathize, trying to understand their journey in my role as the wise guide on the side.

I continually remind myself that every mentee is a unique person with gifts, talents, and strengths to be identified, nurtured, and encouraged—and each person walks (or jogs) at their own pace.

FIVE MENTORING LIFE LESSONS

There are many mentoring life lessons I can learn from my beach walks. Here are five key mentoring life lessons to encourage anyone in a mentoring relationship.

1. *Positive and meaningful face-to-face relationships* are critically important during our learning and self-discovery journey. The mentor as the non-judgmental cheerleader can transform lives.
2. *A positive attitude.* An authentic mentor who smiles through their eyes, has a great sense of humor, and displays compassion and care, is respected and valued by their mentee.
3. *Life is about our choices.* Help a mentee to appreciate that they are unique and their choices can define their future. As mentees develop positive and trusting relationships with their mentors, they become more vulnerable, feel safer, and more secure. Communication moves to a deeper level.
4. *Networks are important.* Help a mentee develop positive networks to support, encourage, and guide them as they seek to fulfil their potential, and find meaning and purpose to their lives.
5. *Promote a healthy and balanced lifestyle* which includes consistent sleep (at least nine hours *every* night for adolescents), regular exercise, a healthy diet, and becoming responsible stewards of the environment.

How do you best reflect on life's meaning and purpose? What can you share with those you mentor?

WEEK 43

A Giant Leap of Faith, or a Moment of Madness?

Remember that clouds color a sunset as much as they bring rain and storm.

What significant decisions have you made in your life? Perhaps you changed career direction, or moved countries? Perhaps you decided to start your own business? Perhaps you were knocked back by a serious illness or accident, and had to alter your career path?

Stories about life-changing decisions can motivate and inspire mentees of any age, as they seek meaning and purpose in their lives. My life story, with all its twists and challenges, has been shared many times in recent years.

A leap of faith? A leap in the dark? All I knew was *that* afternoon I made a life-changing decision.

I sat on a bench in the scenic Kirstenbosch Botanical Gardens overlooking Cape Town on a beautiful summer's day. I was a school principal living my dream. My working life had been spent opposing apartheid, often at the cutting edge of education, wishing to be involved in the inevitable birth of a newly democratic country.

The moment arrived. My school was one of the polling booths for the first democratic election in South Africa—exciting times.

Nelson Mandela had been in power for a couple of years, and was doing a magnificent job transitioning the country from oppression under an apartheid regime to becoming a democracy. There were many challenges, of course, and I had to keep reminding myself that Rome was not built in a day.

One key to creating a thriving country is to have a good education system in place. As a school principal I contributed in a variety of education committees and groups.

That afternoon I was frustrated because almost every time I suggested a positive change in the education system, I hit a brick wall. A few like-minded schools had defied apartheid and opened their doors to students of all races and cultures as far back as 1976, over twenty years earlier. We had much to contribute to an evolving democracy.

My faith was rock solid. I was seeking divine guidance that afternoon.

I looked out over the city I loved, where I had spent over half my life, and heard that still small voice telling me to move to New Zealand.

New Zealand! So far away! Why New Zealand?

I drove home and shared these thoughts with my wife. It's an understatement to say that she was shocked to hear this news and was, initially, unsupportive. Our two children were happily settled in primary school. I knew that by the time they had completed their education and, possibly, further studies, they would find it challenging to find suitable jobs in South Africa.

History had taught me that ten years after a major event—like that which had occurred in South Africa—there would be significant change. That meant "apartheid in reverse," jobs favoring the majority culture (which eventually happened).

During the next eighteen months my father succumbed to cancer, I visited New Zealand to "have a look and see," and then the family enjoyed a Christmas holiday to New Zealand funded by an inheritance.

My wife eventually agreed to put in our applications for New Zealand residency. Our agent told us it would take a few months to process. It took three weeks, and he could not understand why we were accepted so quickly. My leap of faith?

We made plans for the move. I resigned from my job, and was then head-hunted, and asked if I would be interested in another principal's position in Johannesburg. This was a potentially exciting offer, but I was tired and disillusioned, and turned it down.

A GIANT LEAP OF FAITH, OR A MOMENT OF MADNESS?

I flew to New Zealand again for an interview for a principal's job at a small school, and was runner-up. The school later offered me a teaching position. I politely declined, so, when we arrived in New Zealand, neither my wife nor I had a job.

My wife was in tears after our first day looking for a home to rent, and wondered why we had ever left Cape Town—was this leap a mistake? She soon found a job, and the children settled slowly and hesitantly into their new schools after we found a home to rent.

A reputable school principal advised me not to accept "any" teaching job. He felt that, with all my management and education experience, I would quickly become frustrated. I heeded his advice, and remained unemployed.

One thing led to another and I became immersed in the field of youth mentoring, training volunteer adult mentors of teenage students, working for a non-governmental organization (NGO), and developing a national youth mentor training program.

When work began to run out—I still could not find a suitable job in education, winning runner-up prizes by the bucket-load—we decided to take another leap of faith and head to Australia, a decision made easier as our children had completed their schooling.

My first job application was successful. For the next three years I worked for an NGO in New South Wales, developing school-based youth mentoring programs, and running life skills workshops for teenagers.

However, my heart remained keen to return to a school environment, so I applied for an assistant head position of a large co-educational school in Queensland, Australia. My application was successful and, after eight wonderful and memorable years there, I retired.

My son lives and works in Sydney, Australia, in a job he loves. My daughter is a primary school teacher, married with two young children, and lives in New Zealand.

My wife and I decided to return to New Zealand so we could see more of the grandchildren, and we now live happily in a lifestyle village nearby.

Was this leap of faith worth it?

It gave our children freedom of choice to decide where to live, and what jobs to apply for free of any form of discrimination. I sacrificed opportunities to be a leader in education, yet was able to use all my experience to become immersed in the youth mentoring world, and my wife secured jobs relatively easily, though made many sacrifices on behalf of the family.

Later, as an assistant head of a school, I was able to bring all my experiences to a role tailor-made for me. Then, after I retired, I collated my youth mentoring, leadership, coaching and education resources, found a US publisher and have had the privilege of having six books published in as many years.

Faith is described by some as having a firm belief in something for which there is no proof. My leap of faith was filled with calculated risks, yet was life-changing. We miss the beauty of Cape Town enormously, but our decision was without doubt the best for our family at that time. No regrets.

Promoting the spirit of mentoring involves sharing personal stories to encourage mentees to chase their dreams, be prepared to change pathways if necessary, and to remember that there *is* a solution to every challenge.

WEEK 44

Navigating Challenges in the Modern World

Be vigilant with your thoughts. Be mindful of your thoughts, and don't let them consume you.

I am conscious of the global context within which I am writing—now retired and wondering if I have anything worthwhile to offer—and the significant challenges the world is facing.

The COVID-19 pandemic, the lockdowns, environmental catastrophes, the Russian invasion of the Ukraine, the tragedies unfolding in the Middle East conflicts—all have added more challenges to the world of mentoring which will become increasingly important in the next decade and beyond, especially with regard to our youth.

I am reminded that these young people value communicating with mentors or significant adults over the age of fifty. The research states that some of the reasons for this are that these mentors are likely to be settled in their lives, content in their work situations, and happily share life experiences, and that most young people feel safe and secure in the company of this age group.

I look to the future with a spirit of hope.

As I have spent time reflecting on my personal mentoring experiences—over fifty years all in all—while writing this book, I thought of seven key mentoring life lessons (including mentoring qualities) which create a *HOPEFUL* mentor for those who mentor any age, and which can be a source of inspiration or encouragement as we face the unknown challenges in the months ahead.

1. *Humility*: how important it is for mentors to continually remind themselves that the mentoring journey requires humility and honesty at all times. The focus of the relationship is *always* on the mentee and their needs, their goals, and their lives. Great mentors regard mentoring as an honor and a privilege. Once you *connect* with your mentee, you embark on one of the most satisfying relationships in your life as a non-judgmental cheerleader.

2. *Organized*: effective mentoring includes respectfully guiding your mentee to become better organized as they chase their dreams. Management of time discussions are important, with a focus on living a healthy and balanced lifestyle. Coaching goal-setting and the development of innovative, creative, and entrepreneurial skills becomes increasingly important in our post-pandemic global community.

3. *Persist*: the mentor should never give up on their mentee, tempting though this might be on occasions. Effective mentors continually explore different ways to encourage their mentee to reach their potential. Mentors speak to the potential mentees might not see, reach out a helping hand when they stumble and fall, and place them back on the "dream path" with a gentle pat on the back, and a reminder not to quit. Life-changing events could occur, and the development of resiliency is enhanced as mentees master the art of self-learning with the support of a trusted mentor.

4. *Empathy*: the effective mentor does their best to walk in their mentee's shoes. They try to understand *how* their mentee might be feeling. The mentor guides and coaches their mentee *how* to express empathy in their relationships with family, friends, work colleagues, and other members of the community.

5. *Fun-loving*: Mentors create a supportive relationship in which mentees feel cared for, valued, affirmed, and encouraged. Mentors coach their mentee not to take life too seriously, and how to laugh at themselves, skills to pass on to the next generation.

6. *Unity*: mentors promote a sense of unity in their mentee's life, and explore ways of achieving this—family unity, the importance of teamwork, learning how to positively resolve conflicts, and building community.

7. *Listen*: without doubt, one of the most important qualities of a great mentor is to be an effective listener; to show their mentee that their opinions and ideas are valued and matter, and to listen with an open, non-judgmental attitude. Mentors continue to develop the skill of repeating in their own words something their mentee has shared with them, a great sign to their mentee that they are genuinely hearing, and seeking an understanding of what is being shared.

Do I have something to offer?

When I spend time with my grandchildren, I realize that I do. They love the time they spend with us, and we have those special moments when life pauses as I share a golden nugget of wisdom to encourage them on their journey. We laugh lots, and have plenty of fun together.

How effectively are you guiding others to navigate the challenges in their lives?

WEEK 45

Invest Time in Life-Changing Decisions

In times of struggle . . . be still. Be willing to ask for help when you need it.

I was reflecting on the amazing people who reached out to me during tough times in my young life, and guided me closer to reaching my potential. They tolerated my inconsistent behavior, my cheek, my nonsense, my sense of insecurity and self-doubt, mostly hiding my feelings as I recovered from cancer.

Can you remember a moment when an adult invested time in your teenage life and made a positive and significant impact? How did that person encourage you?

What three positive qualities can you remember about them? How did they guide you to be yourself, and not bow to negative peer pressure?

Time and time again I hear stories of the way mentors, often teachers or coaches, have impacted the lives of young people. In many cases the adult had no idea they were having such a positive influence.

My non-judgmental cheerleaders over the years had similar qualities:

- they spoke to the potential in me that I could not see;
- they had a great sense of humor, and taught me not to take life too seriously—and how to laugh at myself;

- they displayed empathy towards me, quietly moved alongside me, and encouraged me;
- they would never accept a half-hearted effort from me, and taught me to strive to be the best person I could be;
- they developed *meaningful relationships* with me, and there was always mutual respect when we interacted.

Without even realizing it, some of these people became significant mentors during my life journey. Those qualities these teachers and coaches expressed towards me are those I have worked hard to develop when working with young people over the years. They gave meaning to some words I came across many years ago, attributed to William Arthur Ward: "The mediocre mentor tells. The good mentor explains. The superior mentor demonstrates. The great mentor inspires."

We often forget the power of the smile, one encouraging phrase shared at an important moment in a vulnerable teenager's life, a friendly wave from a distance, or an encouraging SMS (or message) simply because we think it might be appreciated. These small, seemingly insignificant moments can be life-changers in the lives of young people.

I have guided teenagers to make their own choices, valuing and respecting their ideas and opinions, and telling them that I care about their well-being when they could not understand why I would be interested in their futures. I am still working at patience—so important when journeying with teenagers—though I know I have become a better listener over the years.

I remember some mentoring experiences a few years ago, and how significant these volunteer adults were in the lives of teenagers who were wobbling a little. Perhaps these youngsters lacked self-confidence and, in some cases, displayed the early signs of antisocial behavior—fringe bullying incidents; inconsistent attendance at school, and falling behind with academic studies, as examples.

In one particular school-based mentoring program I was coordinating, the mentors were assisting their mentees to seek some work experience. This was part of the goal-setting journey the mentees undertook to help them find greater meaning and purpose in their lives.

One of the challenges many adolescents have to deal with is fear—fear about making that phone call to the person they want to ask about a possible work experience opportunity; fear because they might be rejected by an employer, or fear because they lack self-confidence, and self-belief; fear because they continue hearing about all the jobs in the future which no-one has heard of yet. Will they cope? Will they qualify for such jobs?

A mentor sat with her mentee as the latter confirmed her work experience opportunity. The mentee phoned the company, and initially had to deal with someone who knew nothing about this.

The mentee was passed on to two other people before she finally got things sorted. She was so happy after completing this process, and acknowledged that she had, indeed, overcome that fear, and how much easier it was having her mentor there to encourage her.

Another mentee became highly motivated about the possibility of teaching as a career, thanks to the work she and the mentor were doing together. Both the mentor and the mentee were bubbling with enthusiasm about their plans for the weeks ahead.

Another mentor was really struggling with her mentee. She felt that they were not connecting. And then there was a potentially life-changing moment.

The mentee, who had been one of those "it's too hard!" youngsters, announced that, since seeing his mentor the previous week, he had organized his work experience. He had also personally sorted out some other arrangements with the Careers Adviser at the school with no help from his mentor, and he shared some other information with his mentor about personal changes in his life.

I observed a young life quietly crossing the bridge to great progress thanks to the persistence of his mentor believing in him.

At a later date that young man thanked his mentor for guiding him and making a significant difference to how he lived his life, set goals, and found a purpose. The mentoring relationship had motivated him to strive to reach higher standards he was setting for himself.

And then there was the young lad who was heading off to work experience the following week. He was pumped and ready to go, and also told his mentor that he would like to stay in touch when the mentoring program officially came to an end.

His mentor also discovered quite by chance, as she was doing some work at her local church, that her mentee attended the youth group there, something he had never mentioned. They later chatted about that, and had a good laugh. It was reassuring to know that the mentee was attending the

INVEST TIME IN LIFE-CHANGING DECISIONS

youth group, as he was mixing with more positive role models, as well as positive peers.

I have shared on many occasions, that one of the key challenges for mentors is *never* to quit on their mentee, and to be motivated, and inspired by author Maya Angelou's words: "I've learned that people will forget what you said, people will forget what you did, but people will never forget how you made them feel."

I mentored a teenager for a year some time ago. She was a wonderful young woman who had been struggling through some personal issues. In recent times she contacted me to inform me that she had made a significant life-changing decision which had been influenced by some conversations we had had during the mentoring relationship.

Do you have a mentoring story to share? Be aware that there is a young person out there who wants to hear it, or another mentor who needs encouragement.

WEEK 46

Insights from a Helicopter Rescue: A Journey of Courage and Growth

Time is more valuable than money. You are enough!

Have you ever quit on a relationship you cared about, or been tempted to do so? Or, has a good friend walked away from a friendship for some reason or other—how did you feel at the time? And now, as you reflect back on that time, any further thoughts?

During one of my morning beach walks, I watched a helicopter rescue someone from the surf, and was in awe of the helicopter pilot's courage and skills. I discovered a short while later that this was a practice, and the person "rescued" was a volunteer from the local surf club.

These volunteers of all ages, shapes and sizes, do amazing work as they ensure the safety of people on the beach, especially as there can be a vicious rip tide to cause panic even from an experienced swimmer at our local beaches.

Swimmers, like mentees, are reassured that there is someone watching over them who is ready to assist should they need help.

I undertook a little research to see what training a helicopter pilot requires to undertake such a challenging job. If I had been walking along the beach with my mentee, we could have undertaken this task together after watching the helicopter rescue take place—a great self-learning opportunity.

Here are a few of the many requirements:

- Strong math skills, including a working knowledge of algebra, geometry, trigonometry and calculus.
- Many hours of training which varies from job to job. Anything from between 45 and 185 hours of training.
- Fifteen written exams and practical tests—the instrument rating is regarded as one of the toughest tests in aviation.
- An understanding and experience in everything involved in carrying out a rescue, such as the preparation and duties of the helicopter's crew, Medivac procedures, rescue basket delivery and retrieval, rescue strap use, dewatering pump delivery, assembly and use.

Do you need any more convincing that this is a skilled job?

The qualities of a skilled pilot are similar to many of those required by a mentor.

Consider only seven of the many characteristics of a good pilot.

1. Responsible—working to help other people requires great responsibility and dependability.
2. Good at organization, planning, thinking logically, and following procedures, which underlines the importance of coaching goal-setting in a mentoring relationship.
3. Excellent at working under pressure—be prepared for the unexpected, and remain calm and focused at all times.
4. The ability to make quick, sound decisions. This is why training is important not just for a pilot, but also for a mentor. One needs to know oneself, and have the self-confidence to be decisive when responsible for the lives of others.
5. A good leader who is able to operate independently in challenging situations. Mentors are role models. Like the helicopter pilot, there are times they need to be discreet, and other times when they must show adaptability. Both display servant leadership as they reach out to others in need of their support.

6. Excellent interaction skills—able to communicate clearly, and build rapport with clients (mentees) and other team members. A skilled communicator is able to relate to people from diverse cultures and backgrounds, so empathy remains a critically important quality.

7. Resiliency—a pilot needs to know their specific strengths which will help them bounce back from a challenging situation that might go wrong. The mentor names and identifies the mentee's strengths as their relationship develops, and encourages the mentee to develop these strengths to reach their full potential.

Other traits required to become a skilled pilot or effective mentor would include flexibility, an innovative and creative mindset, and the ability to positively resolve conflicts.

The pilot, like the mentor, never stops learning and seeks to equip themselves with the most up-to-date training and equipment to do their job to the best of their ability.

The helicopter rescue pilot sets out to rescue people in difficulty, using all their skills and knowledge. The mentor, however, never "rescues" or "saves" a mentee, a key difference in their respective roles.

The mentor moves alongside the mentee and remains the *wise guide* on the side. They coach and teach their mentees how to take responsibility for their life choices, how to chase their dreams, and build a positive network of support around themselves.

There is no quick-fix solution in a mentoring relationship, as every mentee walks at their own pace depending on their personal circumstances.

While there are similar qualities between the helicopter pilot's role and that of a mentor, one of the most important requirements of each role is: "Never quit on the task at hand!"

Have you had an experience when you wanted to quit on someone you cared about? What did you do?

WEEK 47

'If Only I Could Be a Better Parent . . . or Coach . . . or Friend . . .'

Don't let the external interfere with your internal.

"If only . . ." I wonder how many times I heard a parent use these words during my teaching or coaching career?

My journey has involved walking alongside those guiding young people, researching, sharing life experiences, and encouraging people to reach their full potential. I often had to remind them not to beat themselves up, as I shared some proven strategies to create more meaningful relationships with their children, or the young people they were mentoring or teaching.

Have you ever feared the unknown future? Have you ever been through a really tough and challenging situation? A relationship breakdown? Failed an important test or exam? A family crisis? A time you felt you were being unfairly treated? A financial loss? Just missing out on a dream goal? The recipient of an unfair decision? Bullying of any sort?

It seems as though these are some of the issues with which many of today's young people—and many adults—grapple.

They seek meaning and purpose for their lives, want to feel cared for and valued, and struggle with other questions like: What jobs will still be around when I finish school? What jobs will be available to me when

I graduate from university, or further study beyond school? How will robotics and Artificial Intelligence impact my career prospects?

These are legitimate questions and our young people need encouragement and support as they ride the rollercoaster of emotions to discover a future pathway.

QUALITIES AND STRATEGIES TO EFFECTIVELY GUIDE YOUNG PEOPLE

Lou Thompson worked extensively in New Zealand and Australia in the areas of education psychology, behavior management and special needs, and wrote books on developing self-esteem in young people, as well as mentoring youth.

The following twelve qualities and strategies include some of the ideas Lou has shared over the years to help anyone working with young people develop their resiliency and a healthy self-esteem.

I have taken the liberty to expand upon some of them. On further reflection, most of these points could be adapted and applied to anyone moving alongside another person of any age.

- React calmly and constructively to mistakes, errors, and disappointments.
- Overcome setbacks and adversities—be solutions focused.
- Display confidence in your interpersonal relationships—your ability to make friends, and maintain friendships.
- Have a greater belief in your ability to achieve your goals.
- Set yourself specific, realistic, and achievable personal best goals.
- Persevere at striving for your goals in both the good and the bad times, and celebrate the small victories.
- Be prepared to take "acceptable risks"—engage in tasks you haven't attempted before; tackle old tasks in novel ways; engage in tasks where there is a good chance you might fail—a comfort zone is a zero progress, zero growth zone.
- You are less likely to be inhibited in your performance by an underlying fear of failure, as you learn that failure is part of the self-discovery, and self-learning journey. Lou Thompson comments that:

Performance Behavior Children with a healthy self-esteem are most likely to utilize their top 10–20% of potential. They freely move out of their performance 'comfort zones' and in doing so are willing to take acceptable risks. By taking these acceptable risks, they are prepared to attempt tasks they perceive that they might fail at and, additionally, they are willing to undertake tasks that are entirely new. The performance of a child with healthy self-esteem will not be hindered by an underlying 'fear of failure'.[1]

- Respect your health, and have a healthy body image and lifestyle, which includes the responsible use of technology.

    One study funded by the Swedish Council for Working Life and Social Research found that a sample group of more than four thousand young adults between the ages of twenty and twenty-four who were addicted to their smartphones got less sleep, felt less connected to their community at school, and were more likely to show signs of depression.
    —Hector Garcia and Francesc Miralles[2]

- Be able to resolve conflicts positively because you understand that conflict has a positive value. When handled constructively, conflict helps you to learn new and better ways to respond to problems and challenges, build more significant relationships, and learn more about yourself and others.
- Be able to communicate your "real self" to others assertively, knowing when and how to be vulnerable.

This is also a helpful checklist for mentors (and parents), as it will ensure that a young person experiences a holistic mentoring journey as they look for answers to the many questions they ask as their brain develops.

Turn every parenting and mentoring experience into a learning opportunity.

Remember to comment on the young person's *efforts*, refrain from making judgmental comments aimed at the character of the mentee, and you will build new levels of trust.

Work with young people to find creative solutions to the challenges they face, and name and identify their strengths. Teach resourcefulness,

1. Thompson, *Self-Esteem*.
2. Garcia and Miralles, *Ikigai*.

and how to develop a resilient approach to life, as well as prepare them for their career pathways beyond school.

Remember, too, that their attention span is limited, as pointed out by Asheesh Advani: "Between 2004 and today, the average person's attention span shrank from two-and-a-half minutes to around forty-five seconds."[3]

Guide young people towards self-trust—belief and confidence in their ability to face and master difficulties and challenges, and to bounce back with a positive, resilient attitude, and mindset.

Always carry the flame of the mentor's spirit—an affirming influence, combined with positive energy—and you can transform the lives of young people. Instead of feeling fear, these young people will step out confidently into the unknown future equipped with the skills to deal with any challenges they might face.

This is the power of mentoring.

Have you any other tips for the resilient journey to encourage parents, mentors, and coaches?

---

3. Advani and Goldsmith, *Modern Achievements*.

WEEK 48

Secrets Shared for Living a Healthy and Balanced Lifestyle

The one who is swimming against the stream knows the strength of it.

Although I am now retired and, therefore, not facing a possible job loss, or losing my business, I made a *choice* some time ago to take charge of my health and well-being, and to keep looking positively into the future.

I also acknowledge that I am incredibly privileged to live in a lifestyle village, surrounded by friendly people in a relatively safe and secure environment. My wife and I worked hard throughout our careers, and made many sacrifices to be able to afford this lifestyle.

So, my average day follows a loose, flexible structure. Self-discipline is important, as is *choice* of activities. I have been a goal-setter for most of my life.

Annual goals, broken down into monthly targets, give me a focus. They inspire and motivate me to keep on keeping on when I feel like quitting, or permanently retiring from the writing challenges I have set for the year.

During the informal discussions I have with others, especially with young people, I happily share most of these ten ways to strive to reach one's potential. They can be woven into a life skills framework, and adapted by anyone who wishes to live a healthy and balanced lifestyle.

1. Reflection and prayer time: when I wake up in the morning (I am an early riser), I make a cup of tea and spend between forty-five and sixty minutes reading my Bible, reflecting on the daily message and praying. My Christian faith is the foundation of my life, a continual reminder that I *never* walk alone as I seek God's purpose for my day and life. This is the all-important *me time* of my day.

2. This is followed by a healthy breakfast during which time I follow the world news on TV., although I try to avoid being overwhelmed by much of the current doom and gloom news. As a retired history teacher, global news and political leadership fascinate me.

3. Then, if it is not raining, I head off on my approximately seven-kilometer beach walk—a time for further reflection, meditation, prayer, planning, thinking innovatively and creatively, while simply enjoying being at one with nature. I seldom carry a phone or listen to music or anything else while I exercise. I want to experience the beauty of the day. I smile and exchange greetings with others on the beach, not just to be friendly, but because I know these actions release positive "feel-good" chemicals in my aging brain.

4. I return home, shower and, over a cup of coffee, read for between 30 and 45 minutes. This is usually a book that will inspire or motivate me. In our previous home, a friend encouraged me to create an eco-friendly garden, so I added a bird bath and a bird feeder, as well as a bird feeding tray. I fed the birds just before I had my coffee. They were usually waiting for me, so there was this delightful time of interacting with nature. It's more difficult now in the smaller villa in which we live, though on some days it's lovely sitting out on our small deck and just being at one with nature.

5. Thereafter, on most (not all) days, I head into my creating space which can take a variety of forms. Currently I am writing my final book in a series of books promoting the spirit of mentoring, aimed at encouraging others, especially those in the youth mentoring field. I catch up with friends, respond to emails, and try and read ten blog posts a day to be an encouragement to other writers on a social media platform to which I belong.

6. Once a week (on average) I'll head off to a local cafe I support to buy a takeaway coffee and a pie for lunch (my unhealthy binge). This is my small way to support a local business during these challenging

post-pandemic times which have hit the hospitality businesses particularly hard.

7. I make a point of communicating with friends or acquaintances each day, encouraging where I can, or sharing ideas or thoughts about a topic of mutual interest. Or I might write a blog post, always with a message of hope and encouragement. I was encouraged by a reader about my cancer journey which I shared on the *I Had Cancer* website. This reader wrote: "But nothing is too big or too difficult to overcome when applying a positive mindset, have good support structures in place, and unshakeable belief in Jesus Christ our Savior to guide and lead us. Maybe when you wrote it [the blog], you meant it to have a different meaning, but to me it gave me hope and almost a liberation that things will be okay."

8. My wife and I keep in regular communication with immediate family—which includes babysitting our two lovely grandchildren, and having plenty of fun with them—and friends. We laugh lots during these interactions, share our experiences, have some small talk, create cherished memories, and share messages of hope for the future.

9. Either my wife or I take responsibility for the evening meal. I have a more limited recipe folder! Most evenings we eat at the table. Television off. No phones. A time to catch up on all that's going on, share thoughts, ideas, experiences, and future plans. We share chores around the house like cleaning, gardening, or clearing up after meals.

10. Most days I will spend an hour or two tackling a jigsaw puzzle, as I know an activity like this is important for maintaining a healthy brain as I grow older. Or, I'll read a light novel which usually involves positive relationships, as I don't want violence and suffering to cloud my thinking. I also play golf with some good friends twice a week, or return to the beach to fish. The fish love my presence, as they regard it as a free feed. Occasionally—very occasionally—one of them makes a poor choice, and I return home with a meal. We are not immune to those who are suffering, and support charities which are looking after the homeless, or supplying food parcels to the strugglers, or helping others facing tough times.

Everyone will follow a lifestyle that works for them. These ten ways allow me to lead a positive, active life. I never stop learning more about myself, and how I can encourage others.

As I reflected on the content of this post, an article crossed my path. The National Mental Health Commission in Australia was encouraging people to make time for the important things, as this will help us cope with the challenges that lie ahead. I was pleased to read that my list includes their suggested top six ideas to manage mental health:

1. Make time for creativity.
2. Make time for connection.
3. Make time for exercise.
4. Make time for nature.
5. Make time to check in.
6. Make time for yourself.

Most of the content of this post can be shared with young people to encourage them to look with hope at the future; to appreciate that beyond the storm clouds (their challenging times) the sun will shine again; to help them develop their resilience, friendships, and to build a network of support around themselves.

How would you describe your day to your mentee?

WEEK 49

To Love and Be Loved—Every Life Matters

Give more than you take, and see inconveniences as adventures.

Seldom does a day go by without a thought for some of the people who have inspired and motivated me at different times of my life—recovering from cancer as a young boy; moving countries; being in leadership positions, or feeling lonely.

Then I look at the many powerful images of children in war-torn countries shared in the media in recent months, which tug at the heart-strings.

Maybe these images have more of an impact on my life because I was a teacher who witnessed so much in the lives of students whose paths I crossed in a variety of settings.

Nobel Peace Prize winner, Nelson Mandela, is often quoted: "No one is born hating another person because of the color of his skin, or his background, or his religion. People must learn to hate, and if they can learn to hate, they can be taught to love, for love comes more naturally to the human heart than its opposite."[1]

How can we learn to love and reach out to others?

---

1. Mandela, *Long Walk*.

How can we motivate and inspire our grandchildren, children, or other young people with whom we interact?

We can also continually remind ourselves that most young people want to *feel*

- cared for (loved);
- valued;
- that their lives have meaning and purpose.

SEVEN EFFECTIVE WAYS TO ENCOURAGE YOUNG PEOPLE

Here are seven ways to encourage and understand today's young people, gathered from many years of research and personal experiences.

1. Most of today's young people learn best by doing things, reflecting on the experience, and learning lessons from the activity which they can then apply to their daily lives.
2. Young people value and appreciate recognition for their efforts. For example, share a special meal, a positive text message, a congratulatory card, something different in their lunch packs, a surprise of some sort which does not have to cost a great deal of money—preferably none at all.
3. Young people enjoy hearing true stories to which they can relate, and which can motivate, and encourage them to reach their full potential.
4. Young people value learning from older people they respect who are genuine and who *walk the talk*. Such people create an emotionally safe environment in which youths feel secure.
5. Young people enjoy diversity and change. How can we support and encourage them at such times?
6. Young people value *consensus* and *collaboration*, two key words in their world. They need role models to guide them to a deeper understanding of these words.
7. Young people value *clear* and *concise* communication.

    Is there anyone with whom you can connect today?

WEEK 50

Enjoying Positive, Life-Changing Relationships

Remember that you are greater than your problems.

Although I was a teacher throughout my career, I am continually reminded how our young people teach us oldies so much about life. We absorb, refine, reshape, and create these thoughts into "gold nuggets" of wisdom we can share with others.

As we do so, we create cherished memories, and enjoy positive, potentially life-changing relationships with family, friends, and other people with whom we interact.

I stood in the rain watching my grandkids playing hockey. My wife reminded me how important it is to make the effort, despite the weather—I call these experiences "creating lasting memories."

There is doom and gloom in our global community. We are desperately short of global leaders with integrity, who genuinely care and believe that *every* life matters, and who strive, no matter the cost, to see world peace attained.

Sometimes, though not for long, I can feel overwhelmed simply thinking about what needs to happen to transform our global community. The change begins with me, doesn't it?

People ask me why I bother to share my thoughts in musings like these, why I occasionally speak up and swim against the populist flow of incomprehensible and illogical thinking. My response in recent times is quite frankly, "My grandkids deserve better."

I do not want them looking back at these times when they are older, and wondering why their grandparents did nothing to help make this world a better place in which to live. After all, as a teenager I was told, "*You* are the future!"

I watched my eight-year-old granddaughter run in her school annual cross-country. A number of parents were cheering on the sidelines, and I loved how the kids who came in at the end received positive messages of affirmation from their teachers because they had completed the race.

My granddaughter came about tenth last year, and was determined to do better this year. When I was a youngster I ran cross-country, so I offered a word of advice: "When everyone starts walking on the steep hills, do your best to jog slowly. You'll be amazed at how many runners you overtake."

She finished fourth and was quick to tell me that she had run up the hill "most" of the time, with positive results.

In recent times she scored a goal in her field hockey side's victory. She was overjoyed to receive the Most Valuable Player Award—a small hockey stick she keeps for a week, and a pizza voucher (we won't worry about healthy diets)—an award all the players will ultimately receive by the end of the season to promote teamwork.

While my grandchildren like to win, they gain more enjoyment just from running around with their peers than the result. Things will change as they increase their skills, and the competition becomes tougher, though I hope they will always "enjoy" the contest, win with humility, and lose graciously.

I remind them from time to time of one of my life mantras: take a look in the mirror each night and ask yourself, "Have I done my best today?" That's all that really matters, as such a reflection provides some guideposts for the choices we make each day.

SIX MENTORING LESSONS TO ENJOY POSITIVE, LIFE-CHANGING RELATIONSHIPS

When I look at the suffering children in refugee camps, and the faces of children in war-torn countries, I am reminded that positive face-to-face relationships with family (extended family) and friends are critical to enable us to live healthy and balanced lifestyles.

Many millions of young people do not have this privilege, though many of them do appear to be in families that stay together through all the challenges.

I am enjoying watching my grandchildren growing up, and feel incredibly privileged to live within access of their home. As we interact, they continue to teach me these six mentoring lessons that cross all age groups.

1. *Be authentic:* It is important to be myself so my grandchildren know the "real" me—they experience my unconditional, non-judgmental (mostly) love for them; see that I am fallible and will make mistakes; that I apologize when I have done something wrong; that I carry the spirit of forgiveness in my heart, and I never stop learning.

2. *Have a sense of humor:* Laugh lots, be crazy and silly—make a fool of myself (easy to do as a retired teacher). This positive energy releases the "feel good" dopamine in my brain. I must never take life too seriously. Try and find the "fun" element in all that I do.

3. *Listen:* I must not only "hear," but also *listen* carefully for the messages, those feelings, and for what is *not* being said. I continue to learn how to do this consistently with my grandchildren. I remind myself often: "I am the adult. They are children." Sometimes I struggle to empathize, as it was a long time ago when I was under ten years of age. My daughter politely reminds me of this.

4. *Learning is in the doing:* How true this is. We play a variety of games, so I am coaching the seeds of setting and achieving a goal: "Our aim is to catch the ball seven times without dropping it;" teamwork; fair play; perseverance, and learning from failure to achieve the goal. That's how we grow. Lessons we can learn from this activity for our next attempt; sharing small tips about how to throw the frisbee more effectively, and modeling this. They watch, listen, and suddenly they succeed. We celebrate the small victories, usually with a "high five." Never underestimate the power of genuine affirmations, and keep the focus on *effort*.

5. *Develop resiliency:* I can keep coaching my grandchildren how to bounce back when they inevitably stumble and fall. I often use humor,

mixed with compassion, to achieve this. I am always on the lookout for strengths—a quality I consistently can see, and which I will eventually name—as I model the spirit of mentoring in their young lives.

6. *Keep an open mind—variety:* My grandchildren are young, so a game does not last long. Then it's on to something else, then another activity. Then we might take time out to gather our breathe and do some drawing, or read a story, or watch a short movie, or YouTube clip (strict rules around the use of technology), then a jigsaw puzzle, play a card or board game, or play with Lego, or building blocks—a chance to speak to their creativity and innovative thinking. My focus remains on my grandchildren for as much time as possible, and we do what they choose to do (within reason) most of the time.

And, of course, does this particular sentence ever vanish? "I'm hungry!"—because they know Nana Jane bakes lots of special goodies. Sometimes they bake together. But, then, aren't grandparents there to spoil the grandchildren?

And, often there are interesting conversations as we sit around the table and enjoy a meal, or a treat of some sort. They are in a non-threatening, safe and secure environment, learning how and when to be vulnerable.

I am grateful for the opportunity to speak to the potential of our grandchildren which they are often too young to see, and to share messages of hope with young people, especially, who cherish face-to-face healthy and meaningful relationships.

My writing continues, as I share stories, strategies, and tips from my own experiences, and from the multitude of resources I have collected over the years. My hope is that I can raise the awareness that every adult can significantly impact the lives of our young people—and others—with the right attitude and motives.

Like so many others, I am able to breathe life and meaning into Mother Teresa's inspiring challenge: "I alone cannot change the world. But I can cast a stone across the waters, to create many ripples."

How about you? What is your most recent fun family moment? How much fun is it for your employees and co-workers to be a part of your team in your work environment?

How are you reflecting the qualities of a "rippler?"

WEEK 51

With Thanks to an Olympian Who Changed My Life

Focus more on giving than getting.

Stumbling into my hero was a life-changing moment. He was humble, selfless, inspirational, and the best in the world.

I, too, was stumbling and looking for direction and motivation.

When you were young, who was your hero? Do you still have heroes? Who are your guiding lights, the people who have inspired you, and are shaping your life journey?

While walking along the beach on a beautiful day in Autumn—a privilege in my retirement—I was reflecting on all the people who have influenced and shaped my life in positive ways.

I thought about those who have been my mentors and guiding lights during different seasons of my life journey. Names like Peter, John, Pieter, Dave, Tony, Shelagh, Mike and Chris came to mind. Indeed, I have paid tribute to many of these positive influences in my life in these musings, and in my book *Mentoring Minutes: Weekly Messages to Encourage Anyone Guiding Youth*.

One of the people who influenced my thinking and way of living when I was a young adult, and who continues to significantly influence and shape my life and thinking, appeared in the film *Chariots of Fire*, which still rates as one of the best films I have seen.

The film introduced me to one of my "mentors"—definitely a guiding light—I shall never meet, Eric Liddell, the "Flying Scotsman."

I had never heard about Eric Liddell prior to seeing this film. He became my unsung hero, who was an inspirational agent of change in my life, giving me a greater purpose, and the courage and boldness to pursue my dreams.

Eric was born in China to Scottish missionary parents. He was schooled in London, attended University in Edinburgh, and became a dual international sportsman, representing Scotland in rugby and athletics.

Eric was regarded as the fastest man in the world over 100 meters before the 1924 Paris Summer Olympics, yet, on a point of principle—he would not run on a Sunday because of his strong Christian faith—he was unable to participate in that race at the Olympics.

Instead, having come third in the 200 meters final, he ran the 400 meters final and, not only won the race, but also set a new world record which would last until 1936 when it was broken at the Berlin Olympics.

Eric's strange running style saw him running for the finish line with his head and eyes seemingly looking to the heavens. It would be surprising if any athletes and coaches today would refer to his running style as a positive style to emulate. Yet, in the film *Chariots of Fire*, Eric made a simple statement about how he was able to run: "God made me fast. And when I run, I feel His pleasure."

Although Eric ran for a short while after the Olympics, continuing to win most of his races, in 1925 he returned to China as a missionary teacher, eventually marrying Florence Mackenzie with whom he had three daughters.

When World War 11 broke out, Eric decided to send his family to Canada while he remained in China.

In 1943 he was interned by the Japanese at the Weihsien Internment Camp with other members of the China Inland Chefoo School. There he counselled, motivated, and mentored many interns, using his teaching gifts most especially to care for the children.

On 21 February 1945, five months before liberation, Eric died from an inoperable brain tumor at the age of forty-three.

WITH THANKS TO AN OLYMPIAN WHO CHANGED MY LIFE

It remains one of the mysteries of life that so often only *after* one's death people express their thanks, admiration, and appreciation for how that person positively affected their lives.

While this might not have necessarily been the case in Eric's situation, as he was a revered sporting hero who never let these achievements go to his head, the tributes after his death have provided the spirit of mentoring inspiration and motivation for me as a family man, teacher, school principal, sports coach, mentor, and developer of youth mentoring programs—someone who never stops learning.

David McCasland's superb book, *Eric Liddell—Pure Gold,* provides some of the tributes that highlight the spirit of mentoring.

> Never once did he [Eric] show the slightest sign of bad temper or bad sportsmanship on the field; both, it seemed to me, were utterly foreign to him . . .
> —Ted McLaren, teammate in the Scottish rugby team, and a fellow prisoner in China

> Eric is the most remarkable example in my experience of a man of average ability and talents, developing those talents to an amazing degree, and even appearing to acquire new talents from time to time, through the power of the Holy Spirit.
> A.P. Cullen, a friend for thirty-three years

> . . . he won his way through by persistent study, regular time of devotion, constant meditation, insistent prayer, getting up early in the morning and spending one hour—two hours—in a concentrated search for God's will as was revealed in the teaching of Jesus and the Bible generally.
> —A.P. Cullen[1]

One of Eric's roommates in the internment camp, Eugene Huebener, wrote, in a letter to Florence ten months after Eric's death: "Today I am trying to live more like he lived, because he lived like Christ lived."

Another unnamed internee wrote in a personal diary:

> He was not particularly clever and not conspicuously able, but he was good. He was naturally reserved and tended to live in a world of his own, but he gave of himself unreservedly. His reserve did not prevent him from mixing with everybody and being known by everybody, but he always shrank from revealing his deepest needs and distresses, so that whilst he bore the burdens of many, very few

---

1. McCasland, *Pure Gold,* 283–85.

could help to bear his. His fame as an athlete helped him a great deal. He certainly didn't look like a great runner, but the fact that he had been one gave him a self-confidence that men of his type don't often have. He wasn't a great leader, or an inspired thinker, but he knew what he ought to do, and he did it. He was a true disciple of the Master and worthy of the highest places amongst the saints gathered in the Church triumphant. We have lost one of our best, but we have gained a fragrant memory.[2]

The spirit of mentoring involves having fun, remaining humble and selfless, non-judgmental, living a healthy and balanced lifestyle, modeling a strong work ethic, and being compassionate, empathetic and caring.

Eric Liddell personified all these qualities and more. It is easy to appreciate the impact his life journey has had on me, my journey as a cancer survivor, and my career.

One of the pall bearers at Eric's funeral, eighteen-year-old Stephen Metcalf, had helped Eric keep track of the athletic equipment in the internment camp. A few weeks before his death Eric had given his only pair of running shoes to Stephen, saying, "You'll need these for winter."

I think of the spirit of mentoring as walking in the shoes of my mentees—sometimes feeling the blisters, too—to understand them better.

Eric Liddell is an encouragement, though when asked who my hero is—my guiding light—I would think about who Eric Liddell's hero was, and respond: "I follow Jesus." An interesting conversation could then take place as I share my life story.

What about you? Has this story reminded you of someone who has motivated and inspired you, shaped your life, perhaps someone you haven't met either? Who will you share that story with?

---

2. McCasland, *Pure Gold*, 285.

WEEK 52

Always Look for the Magical Moments

Concentrate all your attention on one task at a time.

> Start by doing what is necessary, then do what is possible; and suddenly you are doing the impossible.
> —Francis of Assisi

I switched the sweet (or lolly) from one hand to the other so fast my young granddaughter failed to see this.

"Choose a hand!" I say with a mischievous smile.

She points confidently at the hand that held the sweet.

I open it. Empty.

I open the other hand to reveal the sweet. "Magic!" I say and we both laugh, and she believes I have some magical or enchanting powers.

Will magical moments like this ever end? But I digress.

Do you ever wonder what you will do when you retire? There are so many unknowns ... let me wind back the clock.

Will I spend time babysitting my grandchildren? Or, will I look at ways of contributing to the education debate? Perhaps I can become involved in a program at church, or in the community?

I have this sense that, despite all the technology around us—especially the significant influence (positive and negative) of Artificial Intelligence

(AI)—*positive human relationships* are a key foundation to our future, and must be championed, yet how do I champion that? Or, should I . . .?

The questions continued as I drove out of school for the last time as an employee, and entered the world called "retirement" at the end of March 2017.

What next? Little did I know what would unfold in the months and years ahead.

"You never retire. There's always something to do."

"You will find that you will be even busier when you retire. Well, at least that's what I have found out."

"It is easy to stagnate. I don't want you getting bored."

"I'll never be bored. I have always found something to keep me occupied."

"Remember the old adage: Refire, not retire!"

Voices! Voices! Words of well-meaning advice, caution, encouragement, even concern about my future well-being.

I am seeking words of wisdom and discernment beyond my years as I move away from a world that has embraced my life, and about which I shall always be passionate.

I am looking for what many will describe as a magical moment to transform my life.

Then, one morning, while on my daily walk along the seafront (March 16, 2018, to be exact), a nudge, a voice in my head: "Write a book specifically to encourage Christian teachers. Short, easy to read with lots of tips and strategies to help teachers."

A magical or supernatural moment?

The journey was spluttering to a start. I had many unanswered questions. How could I stand tall in the grace that embraces my brokenness, a fallible, imperfect-by-a-long-way human being, and write a book for Christian teachers?

I had recently collated all my mentoring, leadership, pastoral care, health and well-being, and adolescent brain research, and compiled 260 free *Mentoring Minutes* short podcasts—later, also to become a book—each between two and four minutes in length, as an encouragement to anyone working alongside teenagers.

I had agreed to co-author a coaching handbook linked to a wonderful holistic education self-learning project being developed by well-known author, Dr Jeannette Vos.

And now, this distinct nudge—my magical moment—a message from God that I needed to test because I have to move to a deeper understanding of the meaning of being "faithful."

During the following weeks I wrote a rough introduction to a possible book, able to be read in an hour by a teacher, *HEY TEACHER! YOU ARE AMAZING! 7 Signposts of Effective Change-Agents.*

Then began the journey of testing God's voice, as I sent this introduction to teacher friends, and a variety of teaching associations and organizations in different corners of the world requesting feedback.

Over 90 percent replied, way beyond my expectations, and every response was encouraging, urging me to write this "much needed" book especially for Christian teachers.

But, although I have had other books published over the years, I do not see myself as a writer which, I appreciate, might sound strange to anyone reading this.

I started writing copious notes, capturing ideas, and great quotes which had inspired me over my forty-five-year teaching career, and the ideas for the book began to crystallize. I continued to pray for wisdom and discernment, even writing to a small Christian publisher in Australia asking them if they would be interested in such a book.

They responded and said it might not fit the genre of books they published, yet they felt the book was needed and encouraged me to write it, and send through a copy of the final draft manuscript when it was written. *There* was my motivation.

I asked trusted family and friends to comment on the content as I started writing. One rewrite. Two. Three!

Then a "Wow!" moment, definitely a magical moment on this writing journey.

While my son leads the cheers in the background, my wife and daughter, the latter a primary school teacher, are both my greatest encouragers and critics. As they shared their feedback, I realized that the millennial age group has different responses from the plus forty age group.

"You must be softer, gentler, dad," my daughter advised. "Write as if you were sharing with a teacher face-to-face."

Another magical moment influencing me to be more creative. Major rewrite!

Things were starting to come together. I began to see the light at the end of the tunnel. All the while, I was praying and praying for wisdom and discernment, as I wanted the message to be God's message, using me as His messenger.

"You need to give more information about the personal stories you are sharing."

"More reflective activities would be good."

"I love all the tips and strategies. Teachers will appreciate those."

"Why not ask some teaching friends to share stories you could include in the book?"

Fifth rewrite . . . more prayer, more suggestions . . . sixth rewrite. Nearly there!

Then what can only be described as another magical—other worldly, difficult to explain—moment, the breakthrough!

My wife and daughter approved the content and general tone, and this meant time to check again with some trusted former teaching colleagues.

Positive feedback. More adjustments, tweaks and additions in the seventh rewrite.

Time to seek a publisher and to put on the armor of God (Ephesians 6:10-16) because I call this the "rejection journey." I have traveled the "Thanks, but no thanks!" journey many times over the years.

I also undertook some random googling for publishers who would accept unsolicited manuscripts, as I did not have a literary agent, and finding one just seemed yet another rocky outcrop to scale. On the other hand, was God not my literary agent?

I sent off some proposals and then a friend of mine recommended a couple of publishers, one of which said they would get back to me within six to eight weeks.

In the meantime, the Australian publisher had looked at the draft, liked it, but felt they did not have the contacts to market the book where it needed to be marketed in the education sector. They encouraged me to keep on keeping on.

A New Zealand publisher was keen to work with me on the book, but this was a self-publishing opportunity. While I was grateful for the offer, I did not want to self-publish, as I am a pensioner now, and have to be a wise steward of our finances.

If the voice I heard all those months ago was from God, would He not present the right publisher at the right time? The project was covered with more prayer as the weeks rolled along and the rejections started coming in.

Eleventh hour and about eight weeks from the time I began this publishing journey—I had thrown out the fleece, like Gideon, to God, with an August 31 deadline—that five-minutes-to-midnight *magical* experience.

On August 30 I awoke to find an email from Matt at Wipf and Stock publishers in the U.S. offering me a publishing contract. The working title of the book became: *7 Key Qualities of Effective Teachers: Encouragement for Christian Educators*, and the book was published in 2020.

I believe that we are being challenged more and more each day by an increasingly emotionally driven, secular, faithless, yet influential and powerful media that controls what may or may not be published.

God was telling me it was time to encourage all the amazing, often unappreciated Christian teachers who have a significant responsibility to speak into the lives of youth and their families.

God was also challenging me to shout out unashamedly from the rooftops this very simple message of encouragement to these Christian teachers (indeed, to *all* teachers if they have ears to hear), a reminder that they are *never* alone: "Hey Teacher! You *ARE* amazing!"

Thankfully, God continues to coach me the meaning of being *faithful* to Him—a little reminder nudge that actually I am one of the fortunate to make it through the cancer journey over fifty years ago. He began that coaching way back then, and a little before when I took my first tentative steps to Sunday school at our local church.

Be encouraged to chase your dreams. If they are part of God's plan for your life, He will open and close doors—create what many will call "magical moments"—because His timing is *always* perfect, and often can't be explained.

The journey continues . . .

Post-script 1: One book became six over a six-year period of sharing all my thoughts and resources. Such a privilege.

Post-script 2: I struggle with self-promotion and marketing my work. And then a good friend provided a "magical moment," which my daughter also reinforced. He said:

"You are not promoting yourself, but something you believe in. What you have learnt is worth sharing or it will be lost."

And even though my granddaughters are a little older, we still create many magical moments together. Look for the magic—supernatural, miraculous, charming, enchanting, fascinating, and spellbinding—when you open your eyes and look at the beauty all around you.

I write with a spirit of gratitude to all those who mentored and coached me over the years; who spoke to the potential I often did not see, and who encouraged me to move out of my comfort zone, and use my gifts and talents to create a more positive world.

Share the story of your life journey and those magical moments with your mentees—they will be inspired.

Once a mentor, always a mentor. Never stop being a positive and empathetic role model to young people. Mentoring is a commitment. You invest in the future when you move alongside a young person as their non-judgmental cheerleader.

Create a new story to share with others, inspired by the well-known words of Minnie Louise Haskins, and quoted by King George VI in his Christmas Day broadcast as the world entered the dark clouds of the Second World War:

> I said to the man at the Gate of the Year, "Give me a light that I may tread safely into the unknown."
>
> And he replied, "Go out into the darkness and put your hand into the hand of God. That shall be to you better than a light and safer than a known way."

Appendix 1

Mentoring Matters

The material for Youth Empowerment Seminars (YES!)—now called Mentoring Matters—my community project set up in the late 1980s, has been developed in line with the findings of extensive global research about teenagers which I have conducted for over forty-five years. This research suggests that deep down most adolescents would like the following experiences:

TO BE CARED FOR (LOVED)

- Youth wish to feel safe and secure.
- The more they are cared for, the more secure they feel.
- They wish to be surrounded by people who unconditionally care for them.
- They value the positive influences of peers and adults to encourage them to reach their potential.
- They are encouraged to appreciate that they are more likely to fulfil their potential when there are clear rules or boundaries in place (some of which can be negotiated). When they step over these boundaries there will be reasonable consequences.

TO BE VALUED

- The more youth are valued the more positive self-worth they experience.
- They are encouraged to feel they have some control over things that happen to them.
- Empowering them is proof that they are valued, respected, liked and are regarded as valuable resources.
- They value fun time to interact with peers and adults, which also involves the development of social skills.

TO KNOW THAT LIFE HAS MEANING AND PURPOSE

- Youth want to know that they matter and their lives have significance.
- The more they understand that there is a reason for their existence, the more significant they feel.
- They value encouragement to explore opportunities within and outside of school to learn and develop new skills and interests.
- They are encouraged to acquire a commitment to learning: academic success and the long-term value of learning enhances their self-worth as they discover their gifts and talents.
- They learn to appreciate and understand how to make the tough decisions and choices, and how to cope with new situations.
- They value guidance to develop a positive view of the future.

Acknowledgments

This book is the culmination of approximately forty-seven years as an educator, sport coach, mentor, and youth mentor program developer.

The content of this book, together with other mentoring books I have written in recent years, is a tribute to the many people from a variety of backgrounds and professions who have shared their life experiences and wisdom either with me personally, or with the global community. Many of these people have generously shared their resources with me.

An extensive list of resources is available on my website, providing readers with more references for the content of this book. If I have inadvertently failed to acknowledge a source—which is quite possible, as I have gathered so many quotes and resources over the years—I would be most grateful if the reader would inform me so that I can rectify the omission.

I am grateful to Matthew Wimer and the wonderfully supportive team at Resource Publications, an imprint of Wipf and Stock, who have backed the publication of this book, and willingly guided and encouraged me.

Finally, sincere thanks to my wife Jane—who never believes me when I say, "This is my final book"—for always offering her wisdom and editing expertise without which I would struggle to produce an acceptable final manuscript for the publisher. This *is* my final mentoring book. Much love always!

Bibliography

Advani, Asheesh, and Marshall Goldsmith. *Modern Achievement. A New Approach to Timeless Lessons for Aspiring Leaders.* 100 Coaches, 2024.

Allen, John. *Rabble-Rouser for Peace. The Authorized Biography of Desmond Tutu.* Rider & Co., 2006.

Bailee, Carrie. *Flying on Broken Wings: A Journey of Unimaginable Betrayal, Resilience and Hope.* Affirm, 2014.

Be a Mentor, Inc. https://beamentor.org.8010.

Biehl, Bobb. *Mentoring. Confidence in Finding a Mentor and Becoming One.* Brentwood, TN: Broadman and Holman, 1996.

Browning, Paul. *Principled: 10 Leadership Practices for Building Trust.* St. Lucia: University of Queensland Press, 2020.

Cox, John. *99 Musings of a Dogeared Pilgrim.* Eugene, OR: Resource, 2022.

Cox, Robin. *CHOICES: Encouraging Youth to Achieve Greatness.* Eugene, OR: Resource, 2021.

———. *7 Key Qualities of Effective Teachers: Encouragement for Christian Educators.* Eugene, OR: Resource, 2020.

———. *MENTOR: Strategies to Inspire Young People.* Eugene, OR: Resource, 2023.

———. *Mentoring Minutes. Weekly Messages to Encourage Anyone Guiding Youth.* Eugene, OR: Resource, 2020.

———. *The Spirit of Mentoring–A manual for adult volunteers.* Essential Resources, 2005 (updated 2017).

Du Boulay, Shirley. *Tutu, Voice of the Voiceless.* Hodder & Stoughton, 1988.

Gambone, M. A., A. M. Klem, and J. P. Connell. *Finding Out What Matters for Youth: Testing Key Links in a Community Action/Framework for Youth Development.* Philadelphia: Youth Development Strategies, Inc., and Institute for Research and Reform in Education, 2002. https://www.ydsi.org/YDSI/pdf/whatmatters.pdf.

Garcia, Hector, and Francesc Miralles. *Ikigai. The Japanese Secret to a Long and Happy Life.* Hutchinson, 2016.

Henderson, Nan, ed., with Bonnie Bernard and Nancy Sharp-Light. *Resiliency in Action. Practical Ideas for Overcoming Risks and Building Strengths in Youths, Families, and Communities.* Resiliency in Action, Inc., 2007.

Herrera, Carla, and Michael Garringer, eds. *Becoming a Better Mentor: Strategies to Be There for Young People.* Boston, MA, January 2022. https://www.mentoring.org/resource/becoming-a-better-mentor.

BIBLIOGRAPHY

Jensen, Francis E., and Amy Nutt. *The Teenage Brain: A Neuroscientist's Survival to Raising Adolescents and Young Adults.* Harper, 2016.

Lee, Shen-Li. *Brainchild: Secrets to Unlocking Your Child's Potential.* Independently Published, 2016.

Mandela, Nelson. *Long Walk to Freedom.* Macdonald Purnell, 1994.

McCasland, David. *Eric Liddell, Pure Gold.* Discovery House, 2001.

Morgan, Nicola. *Blame My Brain: The Amazing Teenage Brain Revealed.* Walker, 2013.

Mwaura, Maina. *The Influential Mentor. How the Life and Legacy of Howard Hendricks Equipped and Inspired a Generation of Leaders.* Moody, 2023.

Prooday, Victoria. *The Silent Tragedy Affecting Today's Children.* https://www.yourot.com. Not dated.

Reichart, Michael, and Richard Hawley. *Reaching Boys, Teaching Boys. Strategies That Work—and Why.* Jossey-Bass, 2010.

Reivich, Karen, and Andrew Shatte. *The Resilience Factor: 7 Keys to Finding Your Inner Strength and Overcoming Life's Hurdles.* Three Rivers, 2002.

Siegel, Daniel J. *Brainstorm: An Inside Out Guide to the Emerging Adolescent Mind, Ages 12–24.* London: Scribe, 2014.

Thompson, Lou. *Self-Esteem: Understanding a Complex Phenomenon.* Aber, 2010.

Tyre, Peg. *The Trouble with Boys: A Surprising Report Card on Our Sons, Their Problems at School, and What Parents & Educators Must Do.* Crown, 2009.

Ungar, Michael. Resilience Research Center. https://resilienceresearch.org

World Economic Forum. *The Future of Jobs Report, May 2023.* https://www.weforum.org/reports/the-future-of-jobs-report-2023.

www.ingramcontent.com/pod-product-compliance
Lightning Source LLC
Chambersburg PA
CBHW071715160426
43195CB00012B/1691